A Pictorial

History of

American Crime

1849–1929

ALLEN CHURCHILL

A PICTORIAL HISTORY OF AMERICAN CRIME

1849-1929

Bramhall House / New York

This edition published by Bramhall House,
a division of Clarkson N. Potter, Inc.,
by arrangement with Holt, Rinehart and Winston, Inc.
(A)

Designer: Ernst Reichl

Acknowledgments

THE AUTHOR is especially indebted to Lenore Glen Offord, Lillian de la Torre, and William T. Brannon, all of whom responded with helpful enthusiasm to the idea of the book.

Others to whom the author is grateful are Edward D. Radin, Tom O'Connor, Charles Boswell, Dorothy Gardiner, John Armstrong, John Haverstick, Jean Crawford, George Miller, Edwin Arthur Hill, Helen Decker, Dr. Erik Monberg, Mrs. Margaret A. Koch of La Porte, Indiana; Mrs. Alys Freeze of the Denver Public Library; the Library staff of the New-York Historical Society; Stanley P. Friedman of UPI; Thomas Wheeler of Holt, Rinehart and Winston, and to Ernst Reichl, designer of the book.

CONTENTS

1 Murder in the Medical School—1849.. 3
2 The Unprotected President—1865.... 7
3 Death at the Wayside Inn—1871...... 11
4 The End of Prince Erie—1872....... 15
5 Little Boy Lost—1874.............. 19
6 The Bones of the Merchant
     Prince—1878 22
7 "I Am Going to the Lordy'—1881.... 25
8 The Death of Jesse James—1882...... 29
9 Anarchy and Anarchists—1886....... 33
10 The Man Who Kicked His Wife—1890 37
11 "Lizzie Borden Took an Ax"—1892... 39
12 The Criminal of the Century—1894... 43
13 The Body in the Belfry—1895....... 47
14 The Tattooed Torso—1897.......... 51
15 The Poisoning on the Porch—1898.... 55
16 The Girl in Room 84—1898......... 57
17 Curious Member of a Gentlemen's
     Club—1899 60
18 The President No One Could
     Harm—1901 63
19 Andrew Carnegie's "Daughter"—1904. 68
20 The Girl in the Hansom Cab—1904... 72
21 The Crime of the Century—1906...... 76
22 An American Tragedy—1906........ 80
23 Mike McDonald's Faithless
     Brides—1907 83
24 "Come Prepared to Stay
     Forever"—1908 86
25 Three Sisters in Black—1909......... 91
26 The Plot Against Clarence
     Darrow—1910 94

27 As the Camera Clicked—1910....... 98
28 Finis to a Novelist—1911............ 99
29 An Heiress Vanishes—1911......... 101
30 The Case of the Crooked Cop—1912.. 104
31 Judge Lynch Presiding—1913....... 108
32 Nothing for Something—1913........ 112
33 The Bomb at the Patriotic
     Parade—1916 115
34 Little Charley Fools the World—1919. 118
35 Sacco-Vanzetti—1920 121
36 Death of a Ladies' Man—1920...... 125
37 The Wall Street Explosion—1920 128
38 A Crook with a Sense of
     Humor—1921 131
39 A Comedian's Last Big Party—1921.. 133
40 Hollywood's Mysterious
     Murder—1922................. 136
41 The Clergyman and the Choir
     Singer—1922 139
42 Death of a Butterfly—1923......... 144
43 Teapot Dome—1923............. 147
44 Leopold-Loeb—1924............. 151
45 Two Gentlemen Robbers—1924...... 155
46 Gangland Reigned Supreme—1926 ... 158
47 "Momsie, Momsie, for God's Sake,
     Help!"—1927 163
48 Murder for a Higher Education—1927 166
49 The End of Mr. Big—1928.......... 169
50 The St. Valentine's Day
     Massacre—1929 173
    Bibliography..................... 177
    Index 179

PREFACE

Anyone contemplating a picture history of American crime might think that a varied underworld has been so hidden that few revealing illustrations exist. When, he might ask, did a swindler, kidnaper, thief or murderer ever pose for a camera during his awful deed? Yet pictures of American crime are abundant, some rendering the odd turns and tragic circumstances that surround the law-breaking act, others depicting the actual moment of crime at the very split-second that might be expected to be missing.

When criminals are trapped today, newspaper and magazine photographers (not to mention TV cameramen) swarm in to take pictures. But seventy-five or one hundred years ago, there were no magazine or newspaper photographers, since photos could not be reproduced by the printing press. Instead, there were sketch artists—a designation which may belittle a group of unique talents—who drew for such popular magazines as *Frank Leslie's Weekly, Harper's Weekly,* and the pink-paged *Police Gazette* of hallowed memory. These skillful men freely applied talents (together with pencil or pen) to re-creating the actual moments of crime in famous cases of the day.

If a history of crime can be said to have heroes, these gentlemen are the heroes of this book. Without them, it could never have been done. Therefore, it is annoying not to be able to salute them by name. But for the most part these were anonymous artists, though *Leslie's Weekly* occasionally gave credit to Albert Shults, Albert Berghaus, or Will E. Chapin. The exciting re-creation of Booth leaping from the Lincoln box was done by Berghaus. When President Garfield was shot, Berghaus joined with C. Upham to make a two-man sketch of the assassination scene in the Washington railroad station. Usually, however, the work of magazine artists was printed with the empty credit, "By a Staff Artist." Often these artists sketched from photographs, and one *Harper's Weekly* picture bears this credit: "Drawn from a description telegraphed from Cleveland."

By 1890, newspapers had discovered that, by using extra heavy lines, they, too, could print action and personality drawings. So the field expanded to include newspaper artists who sketched criminals or caught the expressions of witnesses at sensational trials. Some of the top artists of the day—Alonzo Kimball, C. Allen Gilbert, Homer Davenport, M. Stein, Wallace Morgan—did courtroom sketches for New York newspapers. A handsome young man named John Barrymore desperately wanted to be a newspaper sketch artist. For a time he worked on the New York *Journal,* but the competition proved too much and he joined other members of his family on the stage. Or did this intuitive fellow see the handwriting—or the halftone—on the wall? For with the development of the halftone process, newspapers and magazines could print photographs. By 1910, the sketch artist was doomed.

Each reader can decide for himself whether or not this constituted an advance.

All of which is to say that thousands of pictures of American crime do exist, and that many are vivid re-creations. Those selected for this book not only convey the fatal errors of the American past, but often give a vivid impression of the eras in which they took place. The present book concludes with the St. Valentine's Day massacre in Chicago—a crime which terminated one era in the nation's wrongdoing and violently commenced another. With the pictures as a focus, the text allows for a survey of American crime with the salient facts and background of each case. If there is any one factor common to most of the cases, it is the mental sickness inherent in each crime that has caused terrible personal calamities as well as national tragedies.

A Pictorial
History of
American Crime
1849–1929

MASS. MEDICAL COLLEGE.

The ground floor of this chaste-looking building was the locale for the first American crime to attract national attention. The killing of Dr. George Parkman has been called America's Classic Murder.

1849

1. MURDER IN THE MEDICAL SCHOOL

In the early afternoon of November 23, 1849, Dr. John White Webster, goaded to fury, seized a heavy piece of kindling wood and crashed it full force against the head of Dr. George Parkman.

He did this in his laboratory, which was just off the lecture hall on the cellar floor of the Massachusetts Medical College. Next to Harvard Medical School, this was the top institution of its kind in hallowed Boston. Dr. Parkman, who now lay dying, was also a physician (M.D., University of Aberdeen), but some years before, an addiction to money made him abandon medicine for the role of flint-hearted landlord and high-class loan shark. Dr. Parkman had a discon-

certing way of lending money with apparent willingness, suddenly demanding it back with high interest. He was tall and knife thin with a sharp-jutting jaw, and his lean, hurrying figure, attired in stovepipe hat and black frock coat, was familiar around Boston where he was unaffectionately known as "Chin." Yet Dr. Parkman had retained enough sentiment about his former calling to donate the ground on which Massachusetts Medical stood. In return, the grateful institution established the Parkman Chair of Anatomy which in 1849 was occupied by Dr. Oliver Wendell Holmes.

Dr. Webster (M.A., M.D., Harvard) was the opposite. Round and roly-poly, he looked every

3

Dr. John White Webster's pent-up fury made him a match for the taller Dr. Parkman. The murder blow was dealt with the piece of heavy kindling in Dr. Webster's left hand.

inch the absent-minded professor, with spectacles slipping down his nose to bring a look of perpetual surprise to a cherubic face. He was on the staff of Massachusetts Medical and also lectured at nearby Harvard, where he was Erving Professor of Chemistry and Mineralogy. Despite his bemused appearance, Dr. Webster enjoyed the finer things in life, particularly food, wines, and convivial company around a groaning domestic board where Henry Wadsworth Longfellow sometimes dined.

Dr. Webster's combined salaries came to slightly over $1,200 a year and to live so well he had been forced to borrow $400 from Dr. Parkman. He also borrowed $2,432 from a group of lenders of whom Dr. Parkman was one. He made no effort to pay this back, and Dr. Webster's serene belief that the world owed him a living galled Dr. Parkman. He began to hound the chubby doctor, sitting in on Dr. Webster's lectures at the College and making disparaging remarks from a front-row seat. He also persuaded himself that he had been responsible for getting Dr. Webster his position. Then Dr. Parkman learned that Webster had sold his valuable collection of minerals for $1,200, none of which got to him. This provided the last straw and after lunch on November 23rd, Dr. Parkman hastened to Dr. Webster's laboratory.

"Have you got the money?" he demanded, striding in.

"No, I have not," Webster answered calmly.

"I got you your professorship, and I'll get you out of it," Dr. Parkman threatened.

There were more threats, of which Dr. Webster later wrote *I felt nothing but the sting of his words—I was excited by them to the highest degree of passion.* Nearby lay a convenient pile of kindling wood. Short Dr. Webster grabbed a piece and, as best he could, struck tall Dr. Parkman on the head. Top hat and all, Dr. Parkman fell to the floor, bleeding at the mouth.

TRIAL
OF
PROFESSOR JOHN W. WEBSTER,
FOR THE
MURDER
OF A
DOCTOR GEORGE PARKMAN.

REPORTED EXCLUSIVELY FOR THE N. Y. DAILY GLOBE.

PROFESSOR WEBSTER.

NEW YORK:
STRINGER & TOWNSEND, 222 BROADWAY.
PRINTED AT THE GLOBE OFFICE.
1850.

Dr. Webster (also called Professor) could look thoughtful and calm as on the cover of this contemporary account.

For ten minutes, Dr. Webster tried to revive him, using ammonia and other stimulants. Then, as coolly as if he had premeditated the murder (as perhaps he did), the soft little man bolted doors and pulled the body to an adjoining washroom. Climbing into the sink, he hauled the body after him. Jumping back to the floor, he began the grisly task of dismemberment. Oddly, he did not use any of the dissecting knives so readily available, but employed a simple kitchen knife. With the body roughly sliced apart, he put head and smaller sections into a roaring furnace. Other small parts went into a tea chest lined with tanbark. The larger portions were sealed into a vault used for storing the bones of dissected bodies.

Dr. Webster realized that the conspicuous figure of Dr. Parkman must have been observed entering the College, so at the height of the hue and cry over the disappearance, he visited the Parkman home. Dr. Parkman, he reported, had paid him a visit on the afternoon in question, and had left happily after accepting $483 on account. Dr. Webster detailed this plausible story in a nervous, agitated manner. Back at the College, he again behaved curiously by presenting the janitor with a Thanksgiving turkey. This unprecedented act of generosity only aroused suspicion on the part of the janitor, who in his off time began a search of the building. A week later his crowbar broke into the bone vault, where he saw a fleshy pelvis and parts of a leg. He called police, who found the other remains in Dr. Webster's

Dr. Parkman accentuated his thinness by a stovepipe hat and severe attire. Once a doctor, he had turned flint-hearted businessman.

5

laboratory. En route to the police station, the doctor took strychnine, but his nervous stomach refused to hold it.

Dr. Webster's trial was the first to excite America on a national scale. Newspapers as far away as New Orleans devoted columns to it, while one-shot publishers hawked booklets of the testimony, with woodcuts of the principals. In Boston, the courthouse was mobbed. So many clamored to get in that the judge allowed spectators to sit in the balcony for only ten minutes at a time. In this unusual manner an estimated 55,000–60,000 people got a view of the proceedings.

"Not guilty," said Dr. Webster in a strong voice on the first day and he proceeded to brand the Parkman bones a routine cadaver. Because no one had seen Webster strike a blow, the case depended on circumstantial evidence. The unhappy clincher came with positive identification of Dr. Parkman's false teeth, found in the laboratory furnace. At the end of an eleven-day trial, Dr. Webster was found guilty. A few months later he confessed. He was hanged by the neck in August, 1850.

Diagram of Dr. Webster's laboratory shows tea chest, furnace, and sink where body was dissected.

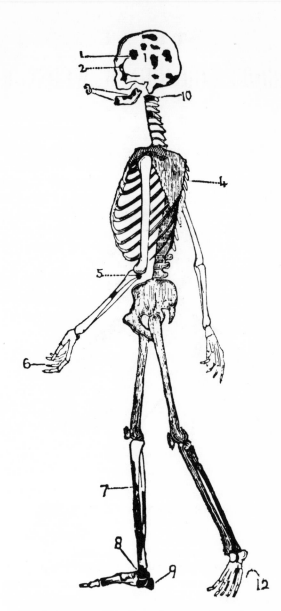

Shaded parts of Parkman's reconstructed skeleton indicate bones found in vault. Black parts were in furnace; others were never found.

6

2. THE UNPROTECTED PRESIDENT

Abraham Lincoln, jogging in a carriage toward Ford's Theater on the night of April 14, 1865, already had eerie premonitions of death. In recent nights his slumber had been disturbed by nightmares about assassination. He even felt that this Good Friday night might be his last on earth and leaving the White House for the thea-

ter, he had said "Good-by" rather than "Good-night" to a favored attendant. Indeed, Lincoln had not wished to attend the performance of *Our American Cousin*, but his wife had insisted. General and Mrs. Grant had been scheduled to accompany them, but had backed out because Mrs. Grant could not abide Mrs. Lincoln. In their

President Lincoln's bodyguard was in a tavern when John Wilkes Booth stole into Box 7 of Ford's Theater, to point his Derringer behind the President's left ear.

Erik S. Monberg

His awful deed done, Booth expected to leap adroitly to the stage, but his spur caught
in the flag, making the leap a fall. A fractured shinbone slowed his getaway.

place the Lincolns had invited young Clara Hale, daughter of a Senator, and her fiancé, Major Rathbone.

In the grip of his premonitions, the President had that afternoon requested a special guard from the War Department. This had been refused—why, historians still are not sure. The only Presidential bodyguard tonight was a shiftless member of the Washington police department. He waited impatiently until the Lincoln party was comfortably seated in the flag-draped Presidential box. Then he hastened to nearby Talta-vul's tavern, where he may have rubbed elbows with another drinker named John Wilkes Booth.

Booth was only 26, but as the son of a famous theatrical family he had already lived a full life. Practically from boyhood, his inherited talents and dashing good looks made him a popular actor. Born and raised in Maryland, he scored his greatest success as a matinee idol touring the

The theater management had provided Lincoln with a comfortable rocking chair for viewing the play.

South, where the easy life and good manners of plantation dwellers made him deem slavery a boon to mankind. Booth had not fought for his beloved Confederacy, but as a popular actor passing the war years in the North, had flaunted Southern sympathies. Single-mindedly, he blamed Abraham Lincoln for all the miseries of the conflict.

Booth stoked vainglorious dreams with potent drink. A man capable of downing two fiery quarts of brandy a night, he talked loudly of kidnaping the President and dragging him in chains to Richmond. Northern armies would then be forced to surrender in order to gain his release. The War Department knew of Booth's drunken boasting, but did nothing. At the same time, he attracted a tiny group of malcontents, of whom he became the proud leader. On March 20, 1865, the kidnap-bent conspirators waited in ambush outside the city limits for the Presidential carriage, but a last-minute change of White House plans thwarted them. On April 9th, Lee surrendered and Booth now swore to kill Lincoln, while other members of his band simultaneously attacked the Vice President and Cabinet members. The actor was in the habit of receiving his mail at Ford's Theater. On Good Friday morning, he overheard the manager say the President would attend that night's performance . . .

At Taltavul's bar, Booth drank until ten o'clock. He knew the play *Our American Cousin* well—when the laughter rose to its height, when the stage was almost empty. He made his way to the theater, stopping to beg a chew of tobacco from a friendly ticket taker. Stealing to the Presidential box—he had examined it that afternoon—he opened the door and crept up behind Lincoln, pointing his one-shot Derringer behind the President's left ear. He pulled the trigger and the small gun banged. As Lincoln slumped, Booth shouted, *"Sic semper tyrannis,"*—(Ever thus to tyrants). Major Rathbone lunged toward him, to be slashed by a dagger Booth had drawn.

The assassin jumped to the rail of the box and began what he visualized as a graceful leap to the stage. "The South is avenged," he shouted, but his spur caught in the flag outside the box and he almost fell on his face. In an instant he was up, to limp across the stage and disappear. The fall had badly fractured his left shinbone.

Without this injury Booth might have made a getaway, crossing the Potomac ahead of pursuers to lose himself among demobilized Confederate soldiers, perhaps reach Mexico. But pain and discomfort slowed him. On horseback he galloped imperiously past the sentry at the Navy Yard bridge and reached Maryland. Here he was met by a conspirator named David Herold, who had failed in a simultaneous attempt to kill Secretary of State Seward. Together the two men located Dr. Samuel Mudd, who put Booth's leg in splints. Mudd gave the names of Southern sympathizers in the region, but none of these dared harbor the fugitives. With Booth on clumsy crutches, they huddled for days in thickets and barns. Booth clamored endlessly for liquor and most of the time was drunk. In lucid moments, he kept a mad diary. On Sunday, April 23rd, they contrived to cross the Potomac, where Booth expected Virginians to greet him with open arms. No Virginian wanted him.

Twelve days after the crime, the two were hiding in a tobacco barn at Garrett's Farm, Bowling Green. Union soldiers approached and Herold plunged out to surrender. Propping himself on a makeshift crutch, Booth waved a carbine and

9

SURRAT.   BOOTH.   HAROLD.

War Department, Washington, April 20, 1865.

$100,000 REWARD!

THE MURDERER

Of our late beloved President, Abraham Lincoln,
IS STILL AT LARGE.

$50,000 REWARD

Will be paid by this Department for his apprehension, in addition to any reward offered by Municipal Authorities or State Executives.

$25,000 REWARD

Will be paid for the apprehension of JOHN H. SURRAT, one of Booth's Accomplices

$25,000 REWARD

Will be paid for the apprehension of David C. Harold, another of Booth's accomplices.

EDWIN M. STANTON, Secretary of War.

THE STATEMENT FROM BOOTH'S DIARY

Friday 21

"After being hunted like a dog through swamps, woods, and last night being chased by gunboats till I was forced to return wet, cold, and starving, with every man's hand against me, I am here in despair and why? For doing what Brutus was honored for—what made Tell a hero. And yet I, for striking down a greater tyrant than they ever knew, am looked upon as a common cutthroat. My action was purer than either of theirs. One hoped to be great. The other had not only his country's, but his own, wrongs to avenge. I hope for no gain. I knew no private wrong. I struck for my country and that alone. A country that groaned beneath this tyranny, and prayed for this end, and yet now behold the cold hand they extend me. God cannot pardon me if I have done wrong. Yet I cannot see my wrong, except in serving a degenerate people. The little, the very little, I left behind to clear my name, the government will not allow to be printed. So ends all. For my country I have given up all that makes life sweet and holy, brought misery upon my family, and am sure there is no pardon in the Heaven for me, since man condemns me so. I have only heard of what has been done (except what I did myself), and it fills me with horror. God,

try and forgive me, and bless my mother. Tonight I will once more try the river with the intent to cross. Though I have a greater desire and almost a mind to return to Washington, and in a measure clear my name—which I feel I can do. I do not repent the blow I struck. I may before my God, but not to man. I think I have done well. Though I am abandoned, with the curse of Cain upon me, when, if the world knew my heart, that one blow would have made me great, though I did desire no greatness.

"Tonight I try to escape these bloodhounds once more. Who, who can read his fate? God's will be done. I have too great a soul to die like a criminal. Oh, may He, may He spare me that, and let me die bravely.

"I bless the entire world. Have never hated or wronged anyone. This last was not a wrong, unless God deems it so, and it's with Him to damn or bless me. As for this brave boy with me, who often prays (yes, before and since) with a true and sincere heart—was it crime in him? If so, why can he pray the same?

"I do not wish to shed a drop of blood, but 'I must fight the course.' 'Tis all that's left to me."

Though drunk during most of his frantic flight, Booth managed to keep a rambling, self-pitying diary. This entry was made five days before capture.

shouted defiance in his rich, actor's voice. "I'll shoot it out with the whole damned detachment," he bellowed. The barn was set afire and he sniffed the smoke. "Well, my brave boys," he mocked, "you can prepare a stretcher for me—one more stain on the old banner."

A shot was fired and Booth fell. Had he killed himself, or been fired on against orders by a fanatical soldier named Boston Corbett? The answer is not known. The Government that had inadequately protected its President also failed to examine the bullet in Booth's dead body.

Shot in the head, Booth was alive when dragged from a burning barn in Virginia by Federal troops.

Erik S. Monberg

Dinner at the Benders often included meat, potatoes—and a sledge hammer. This 19th century rendition has Bender poised behind the canvas partition, his wife serving dinner to the guest, and daughter Kate sitting on the steps.

3. DEATH AT THE WAYSIDE INN

Horror rather than hospitality was the rule of the wayside inn run by the strange Bender family in southeastern Kansas in the years 1871–1873.

The Benders had staked out their claim on a pleasant prairie in Labette County, at a midway spot on the main road connecting the tiny town of Cherryvale and the railroad junction of Thayer. Few houses broke this twenty-mile stretch and the Bender home was a welcome sight to many weary travelers headed for Fort Scott or Indian Territory. The Bender inn was hardly more than a log box, sixteen by twenty feet in size, with an interior unimaginatively divided into sleeping quarters and living room, each sixteen by ten. No solid wall separated these rooms. The dividing wall was merely a loose-hanging curtain of canvas.

Old Man Bender and his raw-boned wife, aged about 60 and 50, were reputed to be immigrants from Germany, but spoke with such gutteral accents that no one could be certain. Two children, apparently born in America, rounded out the family group. The son was a strong, nondescript fellow in his late twenties. Kate, the daughter, was a vivid personality. A vital, high-spirited lass, she was a devout spiritualist who claimed to cure illness and converse with the

11

Kate Bender, only zestful member of the family, continued her lectures on spiritualism despite dead bodies in the family pasture.

dead. Occasionally she gave public séances in nearby Kansas towns and for these, advertised herself as Professor Miss Kate Bender.

All the Benders were big, and it is difficult to imagine them wishing other people inside their box-like dwelling. But with a farm routine established, the Benders opened a general store and wayside inn. In the daytime, coffee and canned goods were for sale to those riding by. By night, travelers were urged to sup at the Bender table or stay overnight on cots. One story says that, for a trifle extra, wayfarers might share the bed of Professor Miss Kate.

The settlers of Labette County saw nothing odd in this. The Benders lived on the main road, why shouldn't they make a few extra dollars? Still, there were whispers. One traveler became alarmed at noises behind the canvas wall as he sat eating with his back to it. Intuition urged him to leap and run, and this he did. Other travelers

reported that friendly Miss Kate became angry and vituperative when a wayfarer refused to sit down with back to canvas.

But no one guessed the truth—that the canvas wall was a necessity for murder and robbery. After a prosperous-looking guest was seated and enjoying his meal, Old Man Bender, the son, or perhaps Miss Kate, found an excuse to visit the bedroom. Next a sledge hammer crashed down on the skull of the unsuspecting man. His body was quickly hauled under the canvas into the bedroom, robbed, stripped, and efficiently dropped through a trapdoor into the cellar. Later, it was buried in the pasture.

After eighteen months of mayhem, the Benders gave one sledge-hammer treatment too many. In the spring of 1873, Dr. William York returned from a visit to his brother at Fort Scott. It was a familiar trip and he told his brother of plans for an overnight stop at the Benders. He was never

12

heard of again. Late in April a worried Colonel York visited the Bender farm. Old Man Bender denied all knowledge of Dr. York, mumbling vaguely of Jesse James and the continuing menace of redskins. He and his son offered to help Colonel York drag a nearby creek. Reassured by this, the colonel galloped away.

For all his Teutonic heaviness, Old Man Bender may have been an intuitive man. Or perhaps Miss Kate blew the whistle. On May 5th, pass-ing neighbors heard the lowing of the Bender cattle. Investigating, they found the inn empty, the Benders gone. As dramatically as in a Western movie, Colonel York now reappeared. Unable to shake off his suspicions, he had returned for a longer look around. He and the neighbors investigated the cellar, smelling a vile odor and noting a thin red crust that could be human blood. Upstairs again, Colonel York looked out over the pasture, where he saw eleven neat indentations.

Neighbors from the surrounding prairie showed up as the graves (RIGHT) were opened. Posses galloped in all directions hunting the Benders, but never found them.

Erik S. Monberg

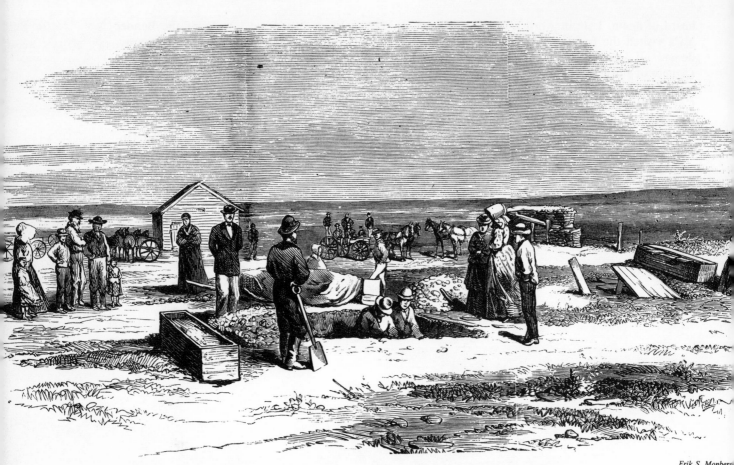

Watchers treated digging as a great spectacle. Later, the ground was probed with iron bars in an effort to locate more bodies. This Harper's Weekly *sketch was made from a photo taken by a local photographer.*

"Boys, those look like graves," he said. They were—the first one opened was that of his brother.

Angry posses set out to scour the prairies for the Benders, and therein lies another tale. The posse which headed south into Oklahoma Territory returned looking grim but satisfied. None of its members ever talked of what the posse had found. This made some Kansans conclude that the posse had caught the Benders and killed them, splitting up murder-profits of an estimated $10,000.

Others thought the Benders got away on the trackless prairie, or boarded a train at Thayer. The search for the Hell Benders, as they were now called, continued sporadically over the next fifty years, with frequent pairs of unhappy traveling females identified as Ma Bender and Miss Kate. In 1889, two women were actually extradited from Detroit on this charge. Labette County was torn asunder, with some residents identifying the pair, while others could not. Evidence became so confused that no trial was ever held.

Jim Fisk started up the stairs, saw pistol-pointing Ned Stokes. He shouted for help, but this famous Leslie's Weekly *re-creation shows that his cry came too late.*

1872

4. THE END
OF PRINCE ERIE

Stokes had lurked at the head of the wide stairway, waiting for his rival in love.

New York's high society thought James Fisk, Jr. crude and vulgar, as did much of Wall Street. But most New Yorkers loved him, calling him "Jubilee Jim." Photos made him look stern and forbidding, but his yellowish-red hair, his bright yellow mustache, his florid face and gaudy attire, always including a diamond stickpin, made him one of the most striking figures of his day. Jubilee Jim was an extrovert, an expansive talker, a belly laugher. He loved life, people, and making money. But most of all, he loved Jim Fisk.

By birth and upbringing, Jim was—of all things—a Vermonter. His father was an itinerant peddler and at age fourteen Jim took the old man aside and told him how best to promote his wares. Within a year, Jim was running the whole show. Word of his success reached Boston, where the Jordan, Marsh Company made Jim an offer. During the Civil War he was the firm's representative in Washington, D.C., winning unprecedented supply contracts by his hearty good fellowship and judicious use of wine and women.

Such a man was destined for New York and flamboyant Jim got to the Big Town soon after the war. In Boston, he left a wife named Lucy, a child of fifteen when he married her. Jim was past thirty when he arrived in New York, as confident of success as a man could be. Wall Street ruled the roost and brash Jim lost no time winning the attention of Daniel Drew, a top robber baron of the day. Through him, Jim met a congenial chap named Jay Gould and the two young men combined to steal the $19,000,000 Erie railroad from Drew. Next, they bought a printing press and printed enough new Erie stock certificates to raise the railroad's value to $57,000,000.

Jim was also hand-in-glove with politicians like Boss Tweed. He worked long hours, and at night liked to mingle with stage folk, especially the girls. He loved tuneful operetta, and bought the Grand Opera House at 23rd Street and Eighth Avenue. Moving the Erie offices into its upper floors, he put the faithful printing press in the basement. The remodeled theater was so magnificent that the public called it Castle Erie. Jubilee Jim was renamed Prince Erie.

Shortly, all New York knew that Jim had fallen in love with a buxom charmer named Josie Mansfield, whose past included a youthful marriage, a quick divorce, a few vague stage roles, and maybe a stint in a bordello. Jim was so mad for Josie that he built her a luxurious home just a few feet from Castle Erie. On Sundays, the two brazenly rode out in Jim's carriage—the most elegant in New York.

If Josie's nights were lively, her days were dull—she was indeed a bird in a gilded cage. She was so extravagant that money seemed to vanish at her touch. With dreams of a lifetime income, she pestered Jim for a huge settlement. Jim made a crucial mistake on the night he brought Edward "Ned" Stokes home to the love-nest for dinner. Stokes was a true patrician, with none of Jim's roughness. One contemporary account calls Ned so handsome it was painful, and women quite naturally found him irresistible. His only flaw was an ugly temper.

Josie's affections quickly swung to Ned Stokes. It took Jim time to catch on, but when he did, the scene rocked Manhattan. To the delight of press and public, all three began a series of suits and countersuits, charging slander, alienation of affections, and blackmail.

On the morning of January 6, 1872, Ned Stokes had testified in one of these suits. Jim's sarcastic lawyer gave him a scorching cross-examination and Ned rushed to Delmonico's for a soothing lunch. There he learned that a grand jury had found him guilty of blackmailing Jim. It made

A hero to New Yorkers, Fisk lay in state at the Grand Opera House as mourners, including an hysterical lady admirer, paid their last respects. His funeral procession, with full military honors, was a notable event.

17

Josie Mansfield, over whom Fisk and Stokes battled, charmed both with a rich Victorian attire.

No longer occupied, the stately office from which Fisk operated had been the scene of multi-million-dollar deals.

the evil temper flare. He leaped up and raced to his hotel to get a four-chambered Colt revolver. He and Josie made a point of keeping track of Jim's movements, and Stokes knew that this afternoon Jim would pay a courtesy call on visitors from Boston staying at the Grand Central Hotel on lower Broadway.

Attired in a red-lined military cloak, top hat, and gold headed cane, Jim arrived at 4 P.M. Starting up the wide staircase, he heard Stokes above him say, "I've got you at last . . ." Jim cried out, "For God's sake, will anybody help me!" But nobody could.

One of Ned's bullets grazed Jim's arm, the other sank into his capacious stomach. Stokes fled, while Jim fell back, stepping unaided down the stairs. Hotel employees helped him up the stairs again and put him in an empty room. Doctors decided that the bullet was so deep in his bowels that operation was impossible. Josie failed to visit the deathbed, but wife Lucy arrived from Boston. "He was such a good boy," she sobbed as Jim expired.

With Josie by his side as a friendly witness, handsome Ned Stokes fought through three trials for murder. At the first the jury disagreed; at the second he was sentenced to hang. A technicality won him a third and at this trial, he got six years for manslaughter. Josie had left New York by the time he got out of Sing Sing and the two never met again. Stokes died a few years after his release. Josie went to Paris and lived until 1931. No one ventured to estimate her true age.

America's first major kidnaping took place in front of this Victorian mansion, the home of the victims, Charley and Walter Ross. Kidnapers lured the two into a carriage.

5. LITTLE BOY LOST

The awful act of child-kidnaping, so familiar in years to come, was all but unknown as the world entered the gentle decade of the 1870's. The disappearance of an angelic-looking boy of four from a quiet lane in Germantown, Pa., on July 1, 1874, brought the terrible crime to national prominence. The boy's name was Charles Brewster "Charley" Ross, and no more forlorn victim appears in the pages of American crime.

Charley and his older brother Walter, six, were lured into a broken-down carriage by two rough-looking men. For five days these men had driven past the roadside spot where the boys liked to play. Each time they stopped to give the little boys candy and exchange chummy words. By July 1st, the Ross boys considered them pals.

When the men suggested a trip to Philadelphia to buy fireworks, the boys accepted. With one of the men taking frequent swigs from a bottle, the carriage proceeded toward the city. At the corner of Palmer and Richmond Streets, it stopped while the men gave Walter twenty-five cents for fireworks. When Walter returned, the carriage was gone.

Walter Ross was led home by a Germantown neighbor who found him weeping on the street. Christian Ross, father of the boys, waited several hours, then visited the local police. No one—police least of all—could believe Charley Ross had been kidnaped. Why pick on the offspring of a man like Christian Ross? True, the Ross home looked imposing, but Ross was no more

19

than a moderately successful grocer. Recently he had gone through bankruptcy and was just on the verge of solvency again.

Yet Charley failed to reappear over the Fourth of July week end. Then, on July 5th, came the first child-ransom note in American history. An illiterate scrawl addressed to "mr ros," it stated that "charlie buster ros" would be returned unharmed, provided the father avoided the police.

Erik S. Monberg

Never seen again, the cherubic Charley Ross was only four years old. His brother, Walter, was safely returned.

Ever a law-abiding citizen, Ross hastened to Philadelphia police headquarters—an act he came to regret. Two days later another note demanded $20,000. Police, still stunned by a kidnaping, began to make a house-to-house search of the city and to check departing ships and trains. Numerous small boys were hauled to police stations, but none turned out to be Charley. The story spread to other cities and produced a pall of horror nearly as great as that of Lincoln's assassination.

The kidnapers corresponded daily. One note said: "we know that you are not worth much money but you have rich friends." Ross was told to collect the $20,000 and lock it in a suitcase.

With it, he was directed to stand on the rear platform of a New York bound train. At a signal from trackside he was to toss the suitcase overboard. As instructed, Ross stood on the train's rear platform. He appeared to be alone, but inside the car lay a clutch of Philadelphia cops. Perhaps the kidnapers knew this, for no signal came from the tracks.

In New York, Ross showed the ransom notes to Police Chief Walling. With amazing speed, he identified them as the scrawl of a petty New York crook named William Mosher, whose brother-in-law was a discharged cop named William Westervelt. Chief Walling immediately enlisted Westervelt's help in locating Mosher. The two held meetings, which produced nothing. Then during the night of December 14th–15th, two burglars were shot rifling a Brooklyn home. In his death throes, one robber confessed, "We killed Charley Ross. We did it for money."

Chief Walling got a peculiar vindication when the corpse turned out to be William Mosher. Little Walter Ross, now seven, was rushed to the Manhattan morgue and, in a grisly scene, identified the bodies as the kidnapers. Philadelphia police, dipping in the New York underworld, promptly heard the rumor that Westervelt had masterminded the kidnaping. Why had Chief Walling failed to hear these whispers in his own bailiwick? Why had he treated Westervelt with such consideration? No one knows—but Westervelt now agreed to visit Philadelphia for questioning. There he was identified as having made inquiries about the financial status of Christian Ross after the crime. In New York a woman rose to recall seeing him in a trolley car with a small boy. Westervelt was arrested and in August 1875 placed on trial as an accomplice. The heavy-set man spoke only to proclaim his innocence, then lapsed into sullen silence. No concrete evidence linked him to the crime, yet the jury found him guilty. The judge gave him seven years in solitary confinement. After serving this grim sentence, Westervelt vanished. . . .

Over the next twenty years, Christian Ross reputedly spent over $60,000 in vain efforts to find his son. He is said to have made trips to examine 273 children, some as far away as Europe. Yet Charley Ross never reappeared, nor were traces of him ever found.

Probably the little lost boy died of grief, fear, mistreatment, or malnutrition soon after the kidnaping, for no fingerprint, lock of hair, or piece

20

"Ros, from yu answer this day yu signify everything is redy. Everything is redy with us, it is left alone with yu whether the boy shall live or die, we caution once and the last time do not think we are trifling. Ros, you are to take the 12 P.M. train tonight from West Philadelphia to New York. it arrives at New York 5.05 A.M. take a cab at Cortland or Desbrosses streets, N.Y., an ride directly to the grand central station at 4th avenue and 42d street. take the 8 A.M. northern express by way of hudson river (take notice) you are to stand on the rear car and the rear platform from the time you leave west phila depot until arrive at jersey city—you are then to stand on the rear of hudson river car from the time yu leave the grand central at New York until yu arrive at Albany. if our agent do not meet yu befor yu arrive in Albany you will find a letter in Albany addressed to C. K. Walter directing yu where yu are then to go. Ros—the probability is yu may go one mile before our agent meets yu and yet yu may go 250 miles before he intercepts yu but be it where it may yu must be prepared to throw the valise to him regardless of all risks. the risk of being lost we assume an you get your child without fail. these are the signals; if it be dark the moment the rear car passes him he will exhibit a bright torch in one hand and a white flag in the other hand, but if it be light he will ring a bell with one hand and a white flag in the other. the instant yu see either of these signals yu are to drop it on the track an yu may get out at the next station, if the cars continue on their course we consider yu have kept your word, and yu child shall be returned to yu safe but if they stop to arrest our agent then your child's fate is sealed. this letter ends all things in regard to the restoration of yu child."

of clothing was ever enclosed in the ransom notes. An underworld story says the kidnapers immediately handed Charley over to Westervelt, who took him to New York. The kidnapers remained in Philadelphia to pen the ransom notes. Westervelt, by this account, grew panicky over the great excitement generated by the crime and drowned poor little Charley in the East River.

The kidnapers wrote notes almost daily to Charley's father. One of the first (ABOVE LEFT), begins "mr Ros—be not uneasy your son charley buster be all writ we is got him and no power on earth can deliver out of our hands." Contents of another note (RIGHT), as printed in the Police Gazette.

William Mosher, who made dying confession.

Joseph Douglass, named as accomplice.

Five months after the kidnaping, two men were killed burgling a house in the Bay Ridge section of Brooklyn. With his last breath, one confessed he and his partner had kidnaped Charley.

6. THE BONES OF THE MERCHANT PRINCE

Burial brought no rest to the remains of Alexander T. Stewart, the first of New York's great merchant princes.

Stewart died in 1876, leaving behind a fortune estimated at $40,000,000, amassed in the classic American manner. An immigrant boy from Ireland, he opened a one-man dry-goods store on lower Manhattan in 1825. "Business was his idol, his pleasure, his profit," an account says. Soon he owned the first department store New York City had ever known. Penny-pinching and avaricious, he was still far ahead of his time in realizing that lavish advertising and promotion pay off. His first big store at Broadway and Chambers Street was such a tremendous edifice that sightseers flocked to it. As the city moved northward, Stewart built at Broadway and 9th Street, the store that later became part of Wanamaker's.

Stewart's two children died in infancy, leaving him and his wife to live alone in a marble mansion at Fifth Avenue and 34th Street. As he grew older, he began construction of a City Beautiful, in Garden City, Long Island. This was to be crowned by the soaring spire of a cathedral built to enshrine Stewart's bones in a polyagonal Gothic crypt. When Stewart died, the Cathedral was unfinished and the dour merchant prince was temporarily interred beside his infant sons in the graveyard of historic St. Mark's-in-the-Bouwerie, at Second Avenue and 11th Street. The crypt was a large, sunken, stone-walled room, with steep stairs leading down. Because the crypt

Thousands watched as the body of merchant prince A. T. Stewart was lowered into a grave at St. Mark's-in-the-Bouwerie. Nearby, reposed Peter Stuyvesant and other prominent New Yorkers.

An immigrant from Ireland, Stewart had amassed a fortune of $40,000,000 after beginning in a one-man store in New York. He developed the first department store in the city.

was airless, the reasoning went, the remains would not decompose and the body was not embalmed.

For two years sparse attention was paid to Stewart's grave. Then, in the early morning of November 7, 1878, the church sexton made a ghastly discovery. The Stewart grave was open! Peering into its dark interior, he smelled an odor "foul beyond description"—evidence that the body had indeed decomposed. Venturing down a few steps, he could see that the coffin had been violated. The grave robbers had unscrewed hinges and chiseled through a lead cover before prying open the coffin top and taking the body, or what was left of it. The vandals had also removed the sterling silver name plate.

News of the outrage spread through the city, and crowds converged on quiet St. Mark's. The investigation was headed by the same Chief Walling whose handling of the Charley Ross disap-

pearance had raised so many questions. "The decomposition of the remains is so offensive," he stated, "that the body cannot be taken across ferries or placed anywhere above ground without discovery." As days passed, the confident words achieved a hollow ring. According to Chief Walling's re-creation of the act, two or three ghouls had climbed a tree and jumped over a spiked wall to enter the locked cemetery. Having opened the grave, they placed the odoriferous body in a sack and hoisted (or threw) it over the wall. Assisting each other, they again used the tree to climb the wall. Three city policemen patrolled the St. Mark's area at night. Yet neither cops nor anyone had seen the body snatchers at work.

Mystery increased as Judge Henry Hilton, executor of the Stewart will, stepped forward to report an attempt at robbing the grave a month before. At this first try the vandals had been unable to lift the heavy stone marker over the crypt.

When informed of this Judge Hilton ordered the marker moved twenty feet away from the right spot. This time, with the heavy marker conveniently out of the way, the ghouls had known precisely where to dig . . .

Some students of the crime suspect Judge Hilton, who is said to have remained calm in the midst of all the horror and indignation. One rumor accused him of supervising the delivery of a large box to the downtown Stewart store, now used as a warehouse. Shortly the box was shipped to Canada. This story gains credence from the fact that in January 1879 Mrs. Stewart received a letter from Canada, offering her the remains for $200,000. The widow Stewart proved as sharp a bargainer as her lamented husband. In a series of iron exchanges, she got the price down to $20,000 and required her correspondents to send her the silver name plate from the coffin as proof that the bones were her husband's. Experts called the name plate genuine. Following this, a young Stewart kinsman drove a buggy through a moonless night to Westchester. There he handed over the money and got in return a gunny sack which when shaken gave off a hollow, bonelike rattle.

Were these the bones of the merchant prince? They were never examined by competent authorities, for the Stewarts decided against an expert scrutiny for fear of discovering they had been cheated. The body snatchers might easily have disposed of Stewart's remains immediately after the robbery, keeping only the name plate, and sold the family anonymous bones.

As soon as the bones reached New York, they were put in a trunk and kept under guard overnight. Again in the darkness, the trunk was placed in a special freight train and carried to Garden City. Here at last it was placed in a special coffin and set to rest in the formidable crypt.

Twice more the eternal sleep of A. T. Stewart was disturbed. With the advent of electricity, an elaborate burglar-alarm system was installed in the Cathedral crypt. Any tampering with the tomb would cause the bells to jangle a strident alarm. Twice—in 1905 and 1908—the alarm sounded wildly. Both times a short circuit proved the cause.

Two years later, the stately graveyard was discovered to have a gaping hole. The ripped-open coffin remained from which Stewart's bones had been stolen.

7. "I AM GOING TO THE LORDY"

Erik S. Monberg

In public the fervent Charles Guiteau never showed regret over killing President Garfield. But in prison cell he was believed to suffer pre-dawn terrors.

Charles Guiteau had the convenient belief that a man's actions are guided from Above. In fact, he felt a special affinity to the Lord, whom he intimately called "the Lordy."

Still, Guiteau was neither a happy man nor a worthy citizen. Dark, slight, catlike, he was thirty-eight but looked ten years older. Illinois-born, he had spent his life pursuing slippery activities. He had been a shyster lawyer; a dead beat whose sharp wits were the scourge of landladies; and an unappreciated evangelist. He had been married briefly to a pretty 16-year-old girl.

After her, he patronized girls of the street with such diligence that he contracted syphilis.

During the 1880 Presidential campaign, the Lord told Guiteau to work for the election of James A. Garfield, so he sat down and wrote a speech which he mailed to the candidate. He also passed out copies at political meetings in New York. Few read the speech and Garfield never delivered it. Yet after the election Guiteau decided that his speech alone had brought Garfield victory. Casting about to find a suitable reward for himself, he picked on the American consulate in Paris. After the inauguration, he moved to Washington to press his claim.

Abraham Lincoln had been assassinated sixteen years before, yet Presidential security had not visibly tightened. A peculiar man like Guiteau was free to enter the White House at will, leaving letters and demands for the Paris job. Presidential aides were first amused by him, then annoyed, and finally infuriated. Once he saw Garfield and spoke to him, but for the most part he preferred to petition Secretary of State Blaine. He badgered Blaine so much in White House corridors that the exasperated Secretary finally shouted, "Never speak to me about the Paris embassy as long as you live!"

It slowly dawned on Guiteau that he might never get to Paris. This was a bitter blow, but he learned how to cope with it. One night the Lord appeared in his sleep telling him to kill Garfield. After that he, Guiteau, would be elected President.

With a 44-caliber British bulldog revolver in his pocket, Guiteau now concentrated on the President. Daily, he sat on a bench across from the White House watching Garfield come and go. When in doubt about the President's scheduled activities, he asked the White House doorman, who told him. Once he stood near Garfield in church, but decided not to shoot for fear of injuring someone else. Another time he held back because Mrs. Garfield—"a dear soul," he thought

Secretary of State Blaine supported a wounded Garfield as bystanders pinned the assassin to the railroad station wall. The President was about to board a train for a trip to Williams College.

her—looked so frail. A third time the weather was too humid for the effort involved. At one point he visited the District of Columbia jail to get an idea of what his accommodations there would be. "An excellent jail," he concluded.

On July 1, 1881 he learned that the 49-year-old Garfield would leave the next day for a visit to Williams College, his alma mater. At 9:20 A.M. Guiteau was lurking in the Baltimore & Potomac station, black hat pulled low over eyes. No one noticed him as Garfield and Blaine entered the waiting room. They strode three-quarters of the way across, then stopped for a few final words.

When they did, Guiteau drew his revolver. Stepping close behind Garfield, he shot into the President's back.

This was perhaps the quietest assassination on record. Presidential guards pinned the assassin's arms and hustled him quickly to jail, where he instantly began penning his memoirs. Garfield was rushed back to the White House. Doctors called the bullet so deep behind his pancreas that (as with Jim Fisk) operation was impossible. Through a fearfully hot summer, Garfield suffered on. In September he was carried to Elberon, N. J., where he died on the 19th.

26

Brought to trial in November, Guiteau was happy at last. The eyes of the world were focused on his trim, fanatical figure. Outside the courthouse, people fought to get in. The judge placed almost no checks on his behavior, and for ten-and-a-half weeks the assassin was king of the courtroom. Leaping to his feet, he made speeches and kept up a vivid running comment on testimony and witnesses. He called the prosecutor an "old hog" and "a low livered whelp." Witnesses were "dirty liars," "low consummate jackasses." The three-ring circus continued each day after court, with crowds moving around to the jail

where Guiteau was allowed to strut before all viewers. After the Christmas holiday he thanked the judge. "I had a very happy holiday," he said. After New Year's, he said the same.

God had told him to kill, he declared. "Let your verdict be, it was the Diety's act, not mine," he urged jurors. He also accused the President's physicians of murdering the Chief Executive. A weary jury sentenced him to die on June 30, 1882. That morning he rose early to shine his own shoes. On the scaffold he sobbed briefly, then straightened to recite a poem of his own composition. "I am going to the Lordy," it began.

Guiteau's megalomania was fully evident on the morning of his hanging. Rising early, he polished his shoes, then shaved with special pride and care.

In an attempt to save the President's life, Alexander Graham Bell was summoned to Garfield's bedside with a new apparatus he had invented. With a telephone connected to the system, Bell listened for a tick that would indicate the location of the bullet. The test failed, but later the machine was perfected and used until the X-ray.

Erik S. Monberg

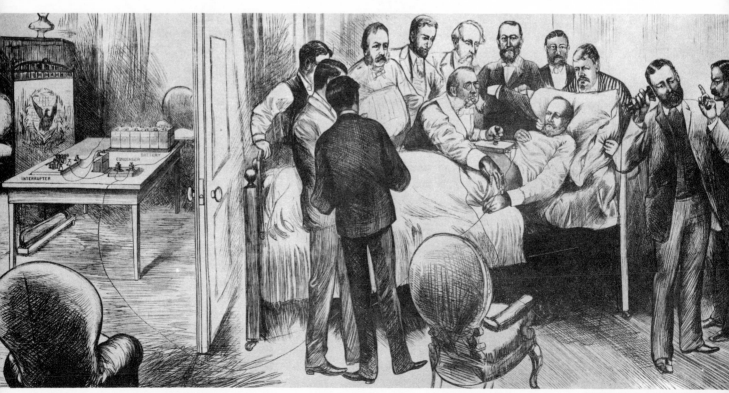

8. THE DEATH OF JESSE JAMES

They forced me into it," Jesse James liked to say when asked how he happened to become Number One Bad Man of the West.

"They" meant the U.S. Government, local sheriffs, and all other forces of law and order, and his reason made a bit of sense. Born in 1847, Jesse grew up in Clay County, Mo., where North and South fought the Civil War in bloody microcosm before the actual conflict. In the Civil War, he was a boy soldier toting a gun for the Confederacy. Back home he remained quiet until 1868, when he was accused of stealing a horse. The charge was false, Jesse swore, and shot two men dead to prove it. From then on he was a wanted man, an outlaw.

Jesse was tall and tough, with a lean face and soft black beard. He blinked constantly, a victim of irritating conjunctivitis. Calm and orderly of mind, he was a born leader of men. Faced with life outside the law, he recruited his brother Frank James and two first cousins, the Younger brothers, forging them into a tight band of expert riders, unerring shots, nerveless killers.

The James Boys quickly perfected the technique of busting a town. First, they galloped down the main street, firing six-shooters into the air. While citizens scrambled for cover, the Boys alighted before the local bank, where they put a gun to the cashier's head and scooped as much as $12,000 cash into sacks. After this, Jesse usually pulled the trigger, leaving the cashier dead. They also held up trains, derailing some, dashing down on others with guns ablaze. First they robbed the mail car, then the lined-up passengers. Sometimes there was a gun fight at the getaway, but the James Boys always managed to escape.

The West spawned numerous others engaged in similar lawless activity but Jesse usually got credit for their acts. For in addition to being a level-headed leader, he possessed the showmanship that makes legend. He was a vicious killer, but dime novels and folk songs glorified his name.

Jesse came to represent the Wild West to the entire world.

For fourteen years he rode high, wide, and lucky. Government troops, silver-star sheriffs, and angry posses hounded his trail. The banks and railroads he robbed hired Pinkerton detectives to find him. Yet the open spaces were wide and Jesse had a chameleon ability to fit innocently into new frontier localities. He married a home-loving girl named Zeralda Minns and fathered two children. For long periods Jesse hid out with his family, under a series of names. Periodically the James Boys regrouped for swift, daring robberies. In 1880 a Pinkerton detective heard the Boys were loose again. Foolishly, he decided to investigate the tip on his own. A few days later his body was found dangling from a tree. On it was a note, "Compliments of the James Boys to the Pinkertons."

So it was war to the end between Jesse and the redoubtable Pinkertons. For a year things went Jesse's way. Then the Pinkertons got a rush of sense to the head. They got the Governor of Missouri to post a reward of $5,000 for the outlaw, dead or alive.

Jesse was currently living as Thomas Howard in a pleasant white-and-green-trimmed cottage outside St. Joseph, Mo. With him were his wife and children, now aged six and three. Neighbors thought him a quiet, non-drinking, non-swearing, churchgoing type. The happy household was completed by Bob and Charley Ford, young men in their early twenties. The Younger brothers had fallen afoul of the law and Jesse was training the Fords to replace them as shooting members of the gang.

When the Fords heard of the $5,000 reward, Jesse's number was up. Yet the trick was to find a moment when the Bad Man was not wearing his six-shooter. Jesse had more reason than any living Westerner to keep his shooting iron on at all times and the Ford boys had to wait for Jesse

to shed his hardware. On the morning of April 3, 1882, the outlaw noted that a picture of his favorite horse, Skyrocket, hung crooked. Stripping off his holster, he mounted a chair to straighten it. Mrs. James and the children were in the next room, but Bob Ford didn't hesitate. Using a silver-handled pistol Jesse had given him, he shot from behind, ripping off the rear of Jesse's head. The Fords then raced to the police.

Henry Wadsworth Longfellow had died a few days before, Ralph Waldo Emerson lay on his deathbed. But the newspapers featured the end of Jesse. The Fords, who had expected to be heroes, found themselves reviled. "A Dastardly Deed," headlined the *Police Gazette*. Other papers approved the death of the outlaw, but could not condone the sneaky treachery of the killing. As usual, a folk song put it best—

> *Oh! the dirty little coward*
> *That shot poor Mr. Howard*
> *And laid Jesse James in his grave.*

The Ford brothers had trouble collecting the $5,000 reward and doubt remains that they got all of it. They went on the stage, appearing in a lurid melodrama called the *Outlaws of Missouri*. Jesse's widow went on a lecture tour. Frank James stood trial, but was never convicted. He became a prosperous farmer and lived until 1915. Jesse James, Jr., who grew up to write a book about his dad. thinks Jesse would have lived peacefully if the law had ever left him alone.

Jesse James, terrifying outlaw of the Wild West, was tall, black-bearded, and personable. In this contemporary drawing, he also had the treacherous eyes of a killer.

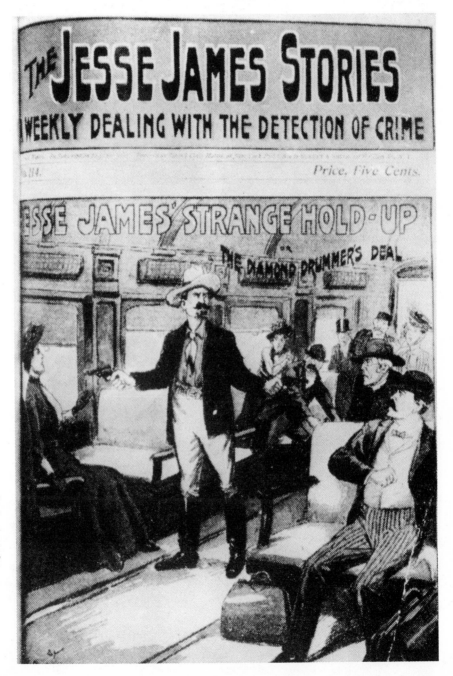

The Scourge of the Frontier rated his own series of dime novels, which in his heyday cost only five cents. On the cover, Jesse nonchalantly held up a train.

The Bettmann Archive

Shot from behind by a boy he trusted—in this inglorious manner Jesse James was finally downed. Longfellow and Emerson died at the same time, but newspapers featured Jesse's sudden demise.

News that their murdered neighbor was Jesse James brought townsfolk of St. Joseph, Mo., on the run. Jesse had a rare ability to fit into a new locality. No one had suspected his true identity.

9. ANARCHY AND ANARCHISTS

Five years after the trial of the so-called Chicago anarchists—accused of exploding a bomb at a Haymarket Square labor rally—a reform administration branded the judge prejudiced, police sadistic, testimony false, jury biased.

Yet at the time few Americans saw anything wrong. Weren't the six accused men labor leaders? Didn't all but one have a foreign name?

plant. Fifteen thousand workers jammed Haymarket Square, listening to the speeches. Suddenly police reserves bore down on the scene, charging and shouting orders to disperse. The crowd fought back and the police struck out with billy clubs, injuring many. A bomb was tossed— no one ever discovered by whom—into police ranks. One policeman was killed and several

Chicago police, firing pistols and waving billy clubs, charged a crowd of labor sympathizers attending a mass meeting in Haymarket Square. The result was a riot and a bomb explosion.

Didn't labor advocate violence in fighting for its rights? Taken together, these factors turned the men on trial into anarchists and bomb-throwers. If they hadn't exactly tossed this bomb, they certainly were capable of throwing another. . . .

It all began at the great Haymarket mass-meeting on the night of May 4, 1886, both a call for the eight-hour day and a memorial gathering for a worker killed four days before in a strike-breaking battle at the McCormick-Harvester

others seriously injured. The cops opened fire and workers with revolvers shot back. In an almost war-size battle, six more police were killed, sixty wounded. Injuries to strikers proved impossible to count.

Throughout the rest of the night, Chicago police conducted an anarchist hunt. Among those hauled in were the labor leaders who had organized the Haymarket meeting—August Spies, Albert Parsons, Adolph Fischer, Louis Lingg, Oscar

33

A war-like battle broke out after the bomb was thrown. Ranged on one side, the police fired on the crowd of 12,000 workers. The workers fired back, killing six policeman and injuring 60. The injured strikers were never counted.

Neebe, Samuel Fielden, Michael Schwab, and George Engel. Booked as dangerous anarchists, these men were jailed and accused of hurling the bomb, though not one of them had been seen doing it.

Chicagoans heaved a sigh of relief. With the city's seven most important labor leaders in jail accused of murder an end might come to bloody industrial strife. Still, a few prominent Americans spoke out in favor of the alleged anarchists. One was the novelist William Dean Howells. Another was the lawyer Clarence Darrow, who here makes his first appearance on the national scene. Newspaper reporters sent to interview the anarchists in prison found themselves on a hot spot. Publishers and editors expected damning stories about the foreign-born men. Yet the alleged bomb throwers seemed (like Sacco and Vanzetti thirty-five years later) gentle, sensitive, and intelligent. One young girl who visited August Spies out of curiosity fell in love with him.

The trial of the men was held in an atmosphere of public hysteria. Testimony from the witness stand tied the men to the bomb, though later it was proved to be the product of police fabrication and bribery. The jury had been questioned beforehand to make sure its members were anti-labor and of the presiding judge the subsequent report said, "Every page of the record contains [his] insinuating remarks, made with the intent of bringing the jury to the belief that the defendants were guilty."

Even so, the case against the men was so muddled that three were given life imprisonment. The remaining five were sentenced to hang on November 11, 1887. The night before Louis Lingg, youngest of the five doomed men, somehow produced a cylinder-size bomb in his cell. Holding it between his teeth he held a candle to the fuse. It blew Lingg to bits and strengthened a frightened public's belief that such men would hurl bombs at others.

On the morning of the execution, Chicago surrendered to terror. Citizens believed that Russian-born anarchists would march on the city en masse, laying siege to the prison in an attempt to rescue the doomed men. Businessmen went to work carrying pistols, anticipating bloody warfare in the streets. Police were edgy, trigger-happy. Yet nothing happened, and the four men were hanged.

Some five years later, in 1892, John Peter Altgeld was elected reform mayor of Chicago. He appointed a committee which uncovered the labor-baiting, sadism, perjury, and corruption behind the Haymarket trial. The Mayor pardoned the three anarchists serving life sentences, thus earning himself the name John "Pardon" Altgeld, which blighted his political fortunes.

But the impression made on the country by Altgeld's pardon was soon dimmed by the attempted assassination of Henry Clay Frick, manager of the Carnegie Steel Company in Pittsburgh. Frick had been left in complete charge of this mighty company while Andrew Carnegie took a vacation. Supposedly Carnegie had gone salmon fishing in Scotland, but it is more likely that he left to avoid a moment of acute labor crisis. Carnegie Steel workers in Homestead, Pa., were angrily striking against a reduction in wages. Carnegie expected Frick to crush this strike by any means, and no one, states author Barbara W. Tuchman, was more competent or willing to do the job. Frick organized a private army of three hundred men recruited by the Pinkerton Detective Agency. In armored barges they moved across the Monongahela. Strikers fought back with homemade cannon, dynamite, and burning oil. With his Pinkerton army stalled by this resistance, Frick appealed to the Governor, who dispatched eight thousand militia.

The labor war along the Monongahela aroused much anger around the country, but still Frick refused to deal with a labor union. On July 23, 1892, he sat in his private office discussing the ugly situation with his chief lieutenant, John Leishman. Outside his office a pale, intense young man entered, showing the receptionist a business card on which was written "Agent of a New York Employment Firm." On this slight basis, the young man was waved into Frick's inner sanctum. He was Alexander Berkman, 21, Russian-born, an avowed anarchist of the bomb-throwing variety, a lover of the notorious Emma Goldman.

Most attempted assassinations are swift and sudden, but Berkman's was long and full of tense drama. One thing which made it so was the fact that Pittsburghers looking up from across the street could easily see into Frick's high-windowed office. Some were actually looking upward at the moment the fiery eyed young man, pulling a pistol, entered Frick's office. As described by W. J. Chamberlin in *Harper's Weekly*, this happened next—

Mr. Frick had been sitting with his face half turned from the door, his right leg thrown over the arm of his chair, and his left elbow resting on the desk. The slight noise [the entrance of Berkman] attracted his attention, and he turned. As he did so, and almost before he had realized the presence of a third party in the room, the man fired at him. The aim had been for the brain, but the sudden turning of the chairman spoiled it, and the bullet ploughed its way into the left side of his neck. The shock staggered Mr. Frick. Mr. Leishman jumped up and faced the assailant. As he did so, another shot was fired and a second bullet entered Mr. Frick's neck, but on the left side. Again the aim had been bad. Mr. Leishman, who is a small man, sprang around the desk, and just as the assailant was firing the third time, he seized his hand and threw it upward and back. The bullet embedded itself in the ceiling back of where the man was standing. . . . Mr. Frick recovered almost instantly from the two shots and ran to the assistance of Leishman, who was grappling with the would-be assassin. . . . The exertion made the blood spurt from his wounds and it dyed the clothing of the assailant.

The struggle lasted fully two minutes. Not a word was spoken by any one, and no cry had been uttered. The fast-increasing crowd in the street looked up at it open-mouthed and apparently paralyzed. There were no calls for the police and no apparent sign of excitement, only spellbound interest. The three men swayed to and fro in struggle, getting all the time nearer to the windows. Once the assailant managed to shake himself loose, but before he could bring his revolver again into play, Mr. Leishman knocked his knees from under him, and the combined weight of himself and Mr. Frick bore the man to the floor. In the fall, he succeeded in loosening one

Four labor leaders, attired in heavy burial gowns of white, were led to the gallows. No direct evidence linked any of them to the Haymarket bomb.

Erik S. Monberg

35

Henry Clay Frick, board chairman of U.S. Steel, sat with his back to the office door when anarchist Alexander Berkman entered, bent on assassination. Shot and stabbed, Frick still survived the dramatic attack.

hand and with it he drew an old-fashioned dirk-knife from his pocket and began slashing with it. He held it in his left hand. Mr. Frick was trying to hold him on that side. Again and again, the knife was plunged into Mr. Frick until seven distinct wounds had been made, and then Mr. Frick succeeded in catching and holding the arm.

At the first sign of the knife the crowd in the street seemed to recover itself and there were loud calls of "Police!" "Fire!" The clerks in the main office recovered from their stupefaction, and rushed pell-mell into the office of their chief. Deputy Sheriff May, who happened to be in the office, was in the lead. He drew a revolver, and was about to use it, when Mr. Frick cried: "Don't shoot! Don't kill him! The law will punish him." The deputy's hand was seized and held by one of the clerks, while half a dozen others fell on the prostrate assailant.

The police were in the office in a few minutes and took the man away. Fully two thousand people had gathered in the street, and there were cries of "Shoot him! Lynch him!"

Frick recovered quickly despite his nine wounds. If any one of them had been half an inch in either direction, vital organs would have been reached. Frick was back at work when Berkman was sentenced to a stiff prison term for the attack. (After serving sixteen years, he was pardoned.) The assault did little to help the cause of labor in Pennsylvania or elsewhere. The still-embattled Homestead workers, it was reported, "generally denounced the act, though some did not seem very sorry about it."

36

10. THE MAN WHO KICKED HIS WIFE

William H. Avery, a Fort Collins, Colo., banker and businessman, was not above kicking his wife.

He did it once at home when she scorched the dinner. At thirty-six, Avery had amassed a fortune of $100,000 from astute transactions in real estate and business deals. Yet returning from a family vacation in the East he bought only a single berth for himself, his wife Mary, and their 14-year-old daughter. Mrs. Avery objected to this uncomfortable economy and he kicked her again.

Six months later the irascible man was dead, following a month of excruciating intestinal agony and horrendous thirst. The day was June 2, 1890, and just two weeks later Mary Avery ran off to become the bride of Frank C. Millington, a dashing fellow equipped with sideburns and a glistening mustache. Millington was ten years younger than his bride, and had been a business partner of her husband's.

The return of the newlyweds to Fort Collins on the Fourth of July provoked a scandal more spectacular than anything in the town's fireworks celebration. Neighbors began to talk openly of clandestine visits made by Millington to the Avery home while Mr. Avery was at work. Avery's brother, president of the First National Bank, heard the gossip and firmly stated his belief that Avery had died of poison administered by his wife and Millington. The bank president secured an order to exhume the body and a coroner's jury was called to assess the findings.

Fort Collins seethed in such turmoil that the proceedings were held in the local opera house, usually reserved for touring performances of *Rip Van Winkle* and other American classics. Mary

Denver Public Library Western Collection

Mrs. Mary Avery had a husband who had a habit of kicking her and a clandestine suitor named Frank Millington.

When Mary's husband suddenly died, she married Frank. The ensuing gossip provoked Colorado's most sensational murder trial.

The Rush for Seats

Excitement at the Millington trial rose so high that a Rocky Mountain News *artist set about satirizing it —one of the few instances where levity entered a murder case.*

Couldn't Find a Seat

Millington, plump and pretty in a matronly way, testified that her late husband was aware of her love for Millington. He had agreed to a divorce and promised her a $30,000 settlement. Why this amicable arrangement had not been completed was never suitably explained.

One batch of doctors swore that Avery's exhumed body showed traces of poison. Others, testifying for the Millingtons, claimed that sulphuric acid poured over the viscera to kill the death-odor had contained arsenic. Avery, they stated, had died of acute gastritis, an aggravated form of a lifelong ailment. Shocking testimony came from a succession of Avery maids who told of Millington lolling comfortably around the premises and even assisting Mrs. Avery to dress. One night, a maid swore, Millington's 18-year-old sister Dillie appeared at the back door disguised as an old hag. Stealing upstairs, she handed Mrs. Avery a large pocketbook. The next day Avery became ill. Presumably the bag contained poison.

The coroner's jury was much impressed by this, and ordered the Millingtons and Dillie held on a charge of administering a fatal poison. Fort Collins was so aroused by it all that a rare change of venue was ordered. Denver was picked as the scene of the trial and here also excitement soared. The large Chamber of Commerce building was selected as the only place big enough to hold the spectators. The over-all Millington defense claimed that the couple was really standing trial for scandalous behavior, rather than murder. Crowds converging on the Denver courthouse bore this out. Men and women battled for a glimpse of middle-aged Mary and her younger spouse. To the State of Colorado, these two represented Scarlet Sin.

The trial was far from scandalous. Medical testimony, long and learned, took up most of the time. Dr. Walter S. Haines of Chicago testified (for a fee of $7,500) that on a second exhumation of the body he extracted $\frac{1}{26}$ grain of arsenic from a pound of Avery's flesh. This meant the body contained 12 to 15 grains, or enough to kill thirty people. The State abandoned the theory that Dillie had delivered the poison in a pocketbook. Now a chemist testified that 14-year-old Pearl Avery bought a lethal quantity of Rough On Rats from him. This story loomed forbiddingly until Pearl mounted the witness stand. The girl firmly denied that she had ever bought Rough On Rats, and added conviction by stating that she still didn't know what the stuff was.

In all, three million words went into the court record, while crowds hungry for sensation sat numb with boredom at the conflicting medical testimony. The jury was told that, to find the pair guilty, it must decide beyond reasonable doubt that arsenic had been administered by the Millingtons. In addition, the act had to be the result of conspiracy, done with malice aforethought.

The jury couldn't. Not guilty, came the verdict. The Millingtons went free, facing a future which included payment of over $20,000 in legal fees. The marriage could not survive this load added to other strains. A few years later the Millingtons split up and soon after, Mary died a natural death.

Effect of Long Stories on Visitors.

Lizzie Borden listened attentively as her lawyer, ex-Gov. Robinson of Massachusetts, argued her case. Though acquitted, rumor, suspicion, and verse indicted her for her whole life.

1892

11. "LIZZIE BORDEN TOOK AN AX"

Borden home was gloomy outside and in. At rear is the barn where Lizzie claimed to have been at the murder hour of 11 A.M.

On the morning of August 4, 1892, the hottest day of a hot summer, Andrew J. Borden, prosperous businessman of Fall River, Mass., consumed a breakfast of mutton broth, leg of mutton, johnny cakes, coffee, cookies, and bananas.

Four hours later the owner of this undisciplined appetite lay sprawled on his favorite living-room couch, hacked to death by blows from an axlike instrument. On her bedroom floor upstairs was the body of his wife, done in by nineteen similar blows struck more than an hour before. The murder of the Bordens in their gloomy home at 92 Second Street, has become America's most pondered crime. Borden's spinster daughter Lizzie, aged 32, was shortly arrested for the killings, and since then the question of her guilt or innocence has inspired novels, non-fiction books, ballads, and even ballets. Even so, the most lasting literary tribute to the case has been a catchy bit of contemporary doggerel which ran—

> Lizzie Borden took an ax
> And gave her mother forty whacks;
> When she saw what she had done
> She gave her father forty-one.

The vast amount of attention beamed on the Borden case has produced little in the way of solid fact. Indeed, it is not actually known if the murder weapon *was* an ax, though the number of whacks can be fixed at twenty-nine rather than the eighty-one of the doggerel. The Borden family circle included Lizzie's older sister Emma, and a maid, Bridget Sullivan. The mother of the two Borden girls had died years before, to be replaced by a stepmother the two spinster daughters never

Lizzie's stepmother was hacked to death in upstairs bedroom. Supposition is that she was approached from behind, struck while on her knees making the bed.

40

liked. Success in business had failed to make Andrew Borden a generous spender and the furnishings of the home were old and depressingly Victorian. The outside doors to the house were kept double-locked at all times, while indoors the family locked their bedrooms throughout the day and carried the keys with them.

On the fateful August morning, older sister Emma was away on an overnight visit with friends (writer Lillian de la Torre thinks she could have returned, murdered, and got back to her friends unobserved). This left Lizzie, Bridget, and a visiting uncle named John Vinnicum Morse who, like Emma, was far from the house between the murder hours of 9 to 11 A.M. The world of 1892 could not believe that an Irish-immigrant maid would dare murder her employers, which left Lizzie the only one in the bolted house with a motive. She and her sister had continued to resent the stepmother and to chafe under the money-tightness of the father—one thing the wealthy man refused to do was install a bathroom. After she reported discovery of the bodies, Lizzie offered a vague story of her stepmother being called out on an errand of mercy. Her father, she said, must have been killed by someone he had crossed in business. Her alibi was that at 11 A.M. she had been in the hayloft of the barn looking for fish-line sinkers. This brought her

Many considered Lizzie Borden a callous, calculating woman. Yet in some photos she appears gentle and sensitive.

Andrew J. Borden was found dead on his favorite downstairs sofa. Tight-fisted with his finances, Borden kept the house in drab, dreary furnishings.

under more suspicion, for who would climb to a stifling hayloft on such a hot day?

But if Lizzie Borden did take an ax to whack father and stepmother to death—how did she do it? The walls of both murder rooms were soaked with blood, but there was none visible on Lizzie or her clothes. Some thought she might have peeled herself naked for the murders. Then, having killed twice, she slipped clothes over her blood-smeared body and called police. But what of the murder weapon? None was ever found, though the Borden cellar held several axes.

Yet suspicion against Lizzie piled up. Police said she had recently made an attempt to buy poison; that she had hinted of a tragedy imminent at home; that she had burned a dress in the kitchen stove three days after the murders. The evidence was all circumstantial, and weakly circumstantial at that. But Lizzie was arrested and, after nearly a year in jail, placed on trial. The nation hung on every word, and to improve their stories some reporters worked to make the evidence against Lizzie appear strong. But it failed to sound that way in the courtroom and a New England jury needed little time to acquit her.

Lizzie never married and after the trial, lived in and near Fall River until 1927. Time neither tied her closer to the gruesome crime, nor did it vindicate her. The fascination of the case, as Edmund Lester Pearson has pointed out, lies in what might be called its *purity*. It seems uncomplicated by greed, lust, ambition, robbery, or other usual murder motives.

The case lives on and only recently blazed into new life. Edmund Pearson was established as its chronicler with publication of *Studies In Murder*, in 1924. This remained the official account until the 1961 appearance of Edward Radin's *Lizzie Borden: The Untold Story*. Radin accused Pearson of presupposing Lizzie's guilt, disregarding and omitting evidence favorable to her. After reading the entire record (had Pearson ever done this? Radin asked) he branded the maid, Bridget Sullivan, the killer.

It all provided a lively controversy, lacking only the presence of Mr. Pearson, no longer alive to defend himself. But through it all the citizens of Fall River acted with equanimity. Most residents of the scene-of-the-crime city think Lizzie did it. Exactly how, they can't say. But in the minds of her fellow townsmen, *Lizzie Borden took an ax....*

Lizzie sat with downcast eyes during most of the trial. Sister Emma, by her side, often covered her face.

12. THE CRIMINAL OF THE CENTURY

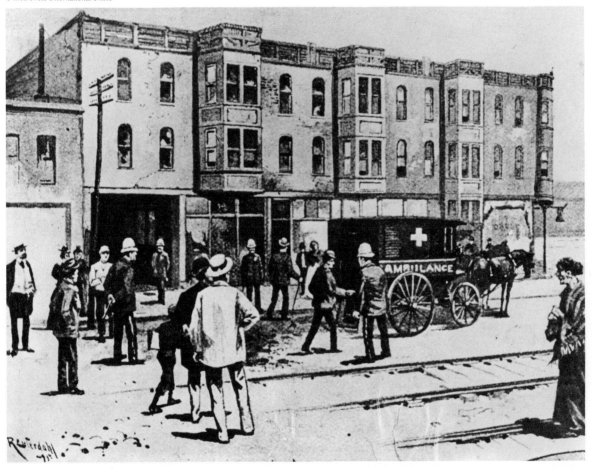

H. H. Holmes, awesome mass murderer, killed most of his victims within this aptly named Murder Castle, at Wallace and 63rd Streets, in Chicago. Interior was a maze of hidden stairways and trap doors.

Harry Howard Holmes was glib and personable. Tall, with mesmerizing eyes and a trim mustache, he killed so many people that beside him the burly Benders seem unimaginative amateurs. He stands forth as America's Number One Mass Murderer with estimates of his victims running from twenty to two hundred. The killer himself modestly pegged the number at twenty-seven. Nearly all his victims were women and, to add a fillip, most were young and pretty. He also killed a number of children.

Harry Howard Holmes wasn't his real name. It was better, he thought, than Herman W. Mudgett, the prosaic name he was given at birth in New Hampshire. He was sharp-minded but lazy in grammar school, and equally so after leav-

Holmes had a sincere, guileless countenance that helped him lure the innocent. Most of his victims were young girls, but he also murdered helpless children.

ing home to enroll in the University of Michigan Medical School. Always his head bubbled with crooked schemes for making money. In medical school he made large sums by taking out insurance policies under different names. Then he would filch a body from the dissecting room of the medical school and use it to cash in the insurance policy. Caught doing this, he was expelled.

Holmes went to Chicago, which became his headquarters in peak years. At first he got along by obtaining furniture on credit and selling it overnight. Moving to another part of town, he did the same thing all over again. After this, he took a job in a drug store at the corner of Wallace and 63rd Streets, in the Englewood section. His knowledge of medicine caused business to zoom. Soon he owned the store, adding a fast-selling line of self-devised alcoholism-cures and get-rich-quick pamphlets. It made sense when he expanded by purchasing the corner plot across the street, but the building he erected there astounded the neighborhood. A turreted, bay-windowed monstrosity, it had almost one hundred rooms. Holmes explained its formidable

44

size by saying he planned to rent rooms to visitors to the upcoming World's Fair of 1893.

Holmes moved his drug store to the street level of the new building, which also had room for other stores. The top floor contained his living quarters—it was the two middle floors and cellar of the odd building which in time earned the name Murder Castle. Holmes hired relays of workmen who worked a few days under his hectic direction, then found themselves fired before learning what was going on. The result was an idiot's-delight of hidden rooms, concealed stairways, trap doors, false walls and ceilings, rooms without doors. One room was asbestos-lined. From it a chute for bodies slid to the cellar, where Holmes had a dissecting table, a stove-cremator, pits of quicklime and acid. From the walls hung surgical tools. His simplest murder method was to chloroform victims into deep sleep, drop them into the asbestos-lined room through a trap door, and pipe in lethal gas. From here the dead bodies slid to the cellar.

Holmes still seethed with mad money-making plans. Execution of them offered a perfect excuse for hiring a series of secretary-typists. "He liked nice, green girls fresh from business college," an account states. In all he hired about one hundred and fifty girls through local employment agencies and they became his major victims. The terrible man was a charmer, able to hypnotize with his snakelike eyes. Rapidly and matter-of-factly, he

Workmen and detectives who dug up Murder Castle cellar were aghast at number of skulls, bones, and human teeth. Chicago police estimated Holmes had killed two hundred persons.

Minnie Williams was lady of the castle for a year. She and her sister had inherited $20,000 and Holmes killed both to get it.

wooed and seduced, persuading the girls to sign over insurance or savings and make out wills in his favor. Finally came the reward of a whole night spent with Holmes in the Murder Castle. Sometimes he simply butchered the girls rather than go through the rigmarole of chloroform and gas. The confusion of the World's Fair aided him in getting away with so much murder.

45

No man—not even a monster—is an island. Holmes married first in New England, then bigamously in Chicago. He discarded this second wife before moving into the Murder Castle. Yet he liked an understanding woman around while engaged in his fast-moving seduction and murder. For a time his mistress was a woman with an eight-year-old child. Then he met baby-faced Minnie Williams, heiress with her sister to $20,000. He killed mistress and child to make room for Minnie, who reigned as favorite for nearly a year. Then Minnie and her sister were put to sleep. Of course, Holmes got the $20,000.

Courtesy of The New York Historical Society

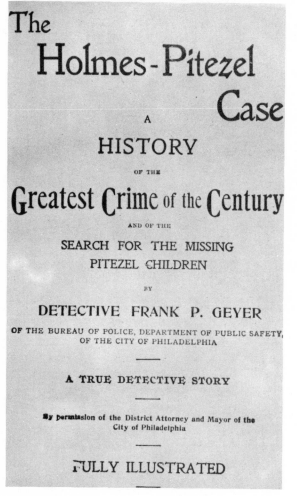

The
Holmes-Pitezel
Case

A

HISTORY

OF THE

Greatest Crime of the Century

AND OF THE

SEARCH FOR THE MISSING
PITEZEL CHILDREN

BY

DETECTIVE FRANK P. GEYER

OF THE BUREAU OF POLICE, DEPARTMENT OF PUBLIC SAFETY,
OF THE CITY OF PHILADELPHIA

———

A TRUE DETECTIVE STORY

———

By permission of the District Attorney and Mayor of the
City of Philadelphia

———

FULLY ILLUSTRATED

———

In all this, he also utilized the talents of a minor criminal named Ben Pitzel, or Pitezel. In November 1893, Holmes complained to Ben that the cost of the Murder Castle had left him $50,000 in debt. He set fire to the building and tried so violently to collect insurance that police suspected him of arson. Rather than allow the law inside, he closed the Castle and fled Chicago.

He began weird travels. During them he murdered; he married a young girl; he landed in a St. Louis jail as a common swindler. Came his fatal mistake. To pass the long hours in jail he cooked up a scheme whereby Pitzel would establish himself in Philadelphia as a prosperous chemist. Holmes would plant a dead body in his laboratory, set it afire and, swearing it was Pitzel, claim $10,000 in insurance Pitzel had taken out. He was so proud of this scheme that he confided it to his cellmate, one Marion Hedgepath. Released in 1895, Holmes hastened to Philadelphia. He had no time for the subtleties of his plan. Instead, he chloroformed Pitzel to death, set fire to the lab, and put in his claim. Pitzel's three young children were sent East to identify the body. To simplify matters, he killed them and made off with the insurance.

This left one loose end. Still in prison, Marion Hedgepath was eager to curry favor. He told the warden of Holmes' scheme. The warden told the insurance company, and Holmes was finished. He was tried in Philadelphia for the murder of Pitzel and hanged on May 7, 1896.

Because he was convicted in another city, H. H. Holmes was never brought to book for his Chicago crimes. Detectives who dug up the cellar of the Murder Castle found so many fragments of skull, bones, and human teeth that the number of his crimes was put at two hundred. Holmes stuck to twenty-seven—quite enough to earn him the title Criminal of the Century.

The title page of book written about Holmes after his conviction.

In this manner the Police Gazette *pictured the first crime of Theo Durrant, who strangled two young damsels in a church in San Francisco. Here he carries the body of Blanche Lamont to the belfry.*

1895

13. THE BODY IN THE BELFRY

Emanuel Baptist Church was the scene of Durrant's crimes. The body of a second girl was found in the blood-spattered church library. Theo was church librarian.

The remarkable thing about William Henry Theodore "Theo" Durrant was his dedication to the Emanuel Baptist Church in San Francisco. He was assistant Sunday-school superintendent, Church librarian, Sunday usher, and hard-working Secretary of the young people's Christian Endeavor. He was also general handyman around the wooden, dull-red edifice on Bartlett Street at 22nd, eagerly fixing broken pews and leaking pipes. To do this, he was given a set of keys which allowed entrance at will to the high-steepled church.

At 23, Theo was an excellent student in the senior class at Cooper Medical College. He was short and slight, weighing only 120 pounds. Yet he was surprisingly strong. His face was long with a sulky expression spoiling a snub-nose boyish attractiveness. Pale skin contrasted sharply with a black, neatly trimmed, adult mustache. A peculiar glaze overlay his bright blue eyes, but not until later did this seem significant. . . .

In all, an apparently exemplary young man. Yet there was talk about Theo. It was said that once he lured a young lady into the church library. Excusing himself for a moment, he reappeared before her stark naked. The girl screamed and fled. Later she told friends, but Theo's fine reputation made it difficult to believe her. There were other whispers about Theo's behavior at church socials. At them, he tried to kiss the girls.

Still, the impetuous youth appeared to straighten up and fly right after meeting dreamy-eyed Blanche Lamont, an 18-year-old high school student who aspired to be a teacher. People usually turned to look at pretty Blanche when she passed and at 4 P.M. on the afternoon of April 3, 1895, she was noticed alighting from a cable car near Emanuel Baptist. Theo Durrant was her escort. Others recalled the couple entering the church. Blanche, it was noted, went willingly.

What happened next? Presumably Theo Durrant led the girl to the church library. He may have slipped out of his clothes again and Blanche may have screamed, or otherwise resisted his advances. Whatever she did, drove him berserk. Putting his hands around her young neck he

48

choked until she was dead. He then hefted the body over his shoulder—or did he drag it by the hair?—and carried it to the belfry, climbing stairs and a ladder. Here he ripped off the clothes. By some accounts he now violated the corpse; by others, he indulged in an unspecified fetish. He then tenderly placed a wooden block, pillowlike under the head and crossed the arms, leaving poor Blanche laid out as if for burial. He went downstairs where he bumped into the church organist, just arrived to practice. The organist remarked that Theo looked queasy. Theo replied he had been fixing a gas jet and inhaled fumes.

As the last person seen with Blanche, Theo had a ready explanation for her mysterious disappearance. He said she must have been kidnaped after leaving him and forced into a house of sin. Such things still happened in San Francisco and this helped soft-pedal the strange disappearance. It also made Theo something of a celebrity. Ten days later he was seen escorting another girl into Emanuel Baptist. She was Minnie Williams, tiny

and twenty-one years old—"a blonde wisp of young womanhood," said the *Police Gazette.* Minnie was known as a gossip. Theo had told her he knew the inside story of Blanche's disappearance.

In the case of Blanche, it is possible that Theo lost his mind on being repulsed by her. Yet medical evidence later showed that tiny Minnie did not repulse him. The two had intercourse in the church library—and still he killed her! Perhaps he told her of the body in the belfry, expecting sympathy. Instead, little Minnie may have threatened to tell police. Whatever transpired, he tore a strip from her dress and rammed it with dreadful force down her windpipe. Minnie died quickly, but nonetheless he grabbed a knife and slashed her wrists, forehead and body, sending a wild spray of blood around the room. He then violated the mutilated corpse.

Next morning, a group of sedate church ladies entered the library to decorate it for Easter. Their screams summoned police who found Minnie's

The killer's hands, displayed on page one of the San Francisco Examiner. *Edited by young William Randolph Hearst, this newspaper pioneered in sensational journalism.*

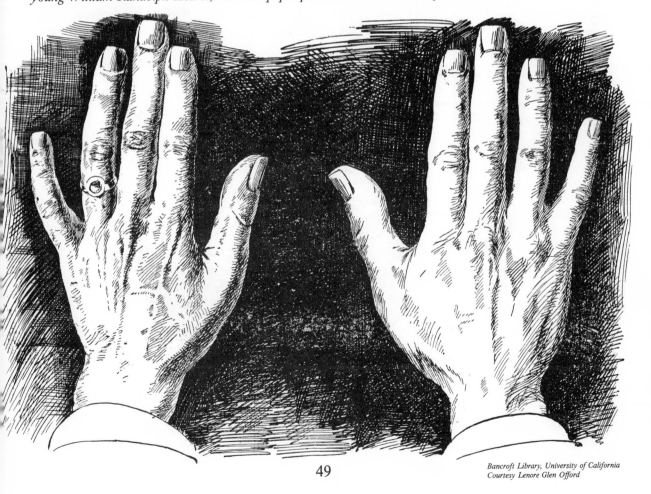

49

body hidden behind a door. A detective then climbed to the belfry where he found the nude, laid-out corpse of Blanche still in a remarkable state of preservation. "The body was white, like a piece of marble," he reported.

So Theo, the last person to be seen with both girls, immediately became suspect. Minnie's purse was found in one of the suits in his closet and gradually a net of evidence enveloped him. Yet he virtuously protested his innocence—it was as if his particular madness allowed him to wipe out recollection of the crimes. His trial was one of the first to be given the "modern" treatment of headlines, drawings, and sob-sister coverage. A "Sweet Pea Girl" presented him with a bouquet at each session and others in addition to this admirer had difficulty seeing the self-possessed young man as a killer. In all, one hundred and twenty-five witnesses testified, among them Theo himself, who thought he made a fine impression on the jury. Yet he was found guilty on the first ballot. Legal appeals ate up the next three years, and not until January 7, 1898, did a composed Theo mount the scaffold. "Don't put that rope on, my boy, until I talk," he instructed the hangman. The hangman went right ahead. . . .

Those amazed by Theo's complacent calm were horrified by the post-hanging behavior of his father and mother. "They seem proud of the whole thing," the warden said of the elder Durrants during Theo's incarceration. With Theo dead, the two waited in a prison anteroom for the body. When it arrived Theo's face was black, with eyes bulging and lips in a grimace which exposed a swollen, bitten tongue. Yet when the warden politely offered food, the Durrants sat down a few feet from the open coffin to consume a hearty late-breakfast. "Papa, I'd like some more of that roast," said Mother Durrant at one point.

San Franciscans were appalled at behavior of Durrant's parents, who seemed to relish their son's notoriety. While Theo hanged, father and mother sat down to a hearty lunch in the death house—with the open coffin a few feet away.

14. THE TATTOOED TORSO

Police stood open-mouthed on the sidelines while newspaper reporters solved the mystery of Willie Guldensuppe, who was shot, stabbed, and hacked to bits, in the rustic suburb of Woodside, Queens, across the East River from Manhattan.

Willie's demise became the battlefield for the first great tussle in New York's incredible war of Yellow Journalism. William Randolph Hearst, leaving San Francisco after the Durrant killings, came to New York where he bought the *Journal.* Using the screaming-headline and fake-photo techniques perfected in the West, he challenged the towering New York *World* to a bitter circulation war. The *World* could have remained aloof, but didn't. It sank to Hearst's level and a wild war began. "Get the story and to hell with the cost," became the motto of city rooms. The Guldensuppe case, in June 1897, was the first big journalistic brawl with no holds barred.

Willie's murder has still another distinction. It is the only mystery on record involving pink ducks. The ducks, roaming free on a Woodside farm, were glistening white one morning in June, that night streaked with red. An astonished farmer investigated, to find his ducks incarnadined by drinking out of a blood-tinted pool fed by a drain from a nearby cottage.

Reporters from the *Journal* and *World*—and to a lesser extent the New York police—had been frantically searching for just such a Murder Cottage. For during the past seven days, hunks of a male body, wrapped in red-and-gold oilcloth had been popping up in the rivers around Manhattan. One grisly package contained a man's legs, another a tattooed torso. The pink pool seemed to provide a clue to their source.

With this, the entire mystery seemed to burst open. A *World* reporter relaxing in a midtown Turkish Bath heard two attendants lamenting the week-long absence of burly, blond Willie Guldensuppe, a fellow rubber. The reporter sat up. "Was your friend Willie tattooed?" he inquired. Yes—a fine female figure adorned Willie's hairy

chest. So the hunks of body were identified. Records at the Turkish Bath showed that Willie lived at 439 Ninth Avenue, a boardinghouse run by German-born Mrs. Augusta Nack, an unlicensed midwife.

Journal reporters, meantime, had been concentrating on the oilcloth. A Queens shopkeeper remembered selling it to a woman of Mrs. Nack's description. Newsmen, rather than the law, now galloped to 439 Ninth Avenue. The *Journal* got there first and fought off *World* reporters. Mr. Hearst's men (MURDER MYSTERY SOLVED BY JOURNAL!) proudly led Augusta Nack to police

When a pool fed by a drain from 346 Second Street, Woodside, L.I., turned red, neighbors called the police, who discovered Murder Cottage.

MURDERER OF GULDENSUPPE, MARTIN THORN, WILL PAY THE PENALTY AND BE KILLED TO-DAY.

Condemned Murderer Is Calm, Says
He Has No Fear, and Is
Sure of Forgiveness.

*Mrs. Nack got ten years for murder. Her lover, Martin Thorn, got the chair. The
New York* World *saw him as a man entrapped by the designs of an evil woman.*

Under stylish garb, Turkish Bath attendant Willie Guldensuppe was a mass of colorful tattoos. When chunks of his body were found in waters around Manhattan, the tattooing hastened identification.

headquarters, where the cops tried shock tactics. The midwife was suddenly faced with the rotting legs wrapped in oilcloth. "Are those Willie's?" she was asked. Mrs. Nack was heavy-set and stolid, but able to affect the grand manner. "I would not know," she answered regally, "as I never saw the gentleman naked."

Her Ninth Avenue neighbors laughed at this. Why, Willie and Mrs. Nack had been lovers for years, they told reporters. Things had been lovey-dovey until a year ago, when a young barber named George Thorn took a room with Mrs. Nack. Soon both men were the lady's lovers. Willie objected, and he and Thorn had several bloody fights. Slowly it became apparent to Willie that young Thorn was the midwife's favorite. Swallowing his sorrow, he began to date other women. This, in turn, exasperated Mrs. Nack, who told Thorn that Willie must die. Or did Thorn decide to murder his rival after a fight? Both stories are on the record.

At any rate, the lovers rented the cottage in Woodside. Mrs. Nack told ex-lover Willie that she planned to use it as a "baby farm" and asked

53

him to render his expert opinion of the premises. On the day Willie visited Woodside to do this, she insisted that he peer into every nook and closet. Thorn lurked in one closet, armed with a revolver, dagger, and bottle of poison. When Willie opened the door, he fired, then stabbed his hefty rival through the heart. The two pulled the body to the bathtub, where Thorn neatly severed the head with his barber's razor. As he sliced away at the rest, Mrs. Nack went in search of oilcloth. Thorn kept the water taps running during his grisly work, believing the plumbing led to a sewer. But there were no sewers then in woodsy Woodside. . . .

With Mrs. Nack in the clutches of the law, Thorn attempted a dramatic getaway to Canada. Brought back, he was faced by a barber friend to whom he had gloatingly described the killing. Once again the Yellow Press took charge, with the *Journal* sending an evangelist named Miles

on daily visits to Mrs. Nack. He wrote the exclusive story of each visit to her cell for the jubilant *Journal.* From the evangelist, Mrs. Nack unexpectedly got religion. On the second day of the trial, she rose to confess in such ghastly detail that a juror collapsed, causing a mistrial. At the second trial Thorn's chance came. He accused Mrs. Nack of plotting the murder. He said the Woodside cottage was only a love nest. One day he arrived there to find Augusta waiting. "Willie's upstairs," she announced, "I just killed him."

With both stories before them, the jury chose Mrs. Nack's. Thorn was sentenced to the electric chair, Mrs. Nack given twenty years to life. An exemplary prisoner, she was paroled in ten. With singular callousness, she returned to her old Ninth Avenue neighborhood and opened a delicatessen. Few patronized it and Augusta Nack, hard-eyed landlady and unlicensed midwife, vanished into the mists of time.

This imposing array of weapons was found in the quarters of Mrs. Augusta Nack, Willie's landlady. Spots on the saw were identified as human blood.

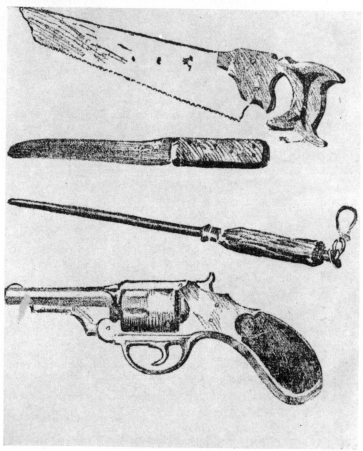

54

15. THE POISONING ON THE PORCH

Bancroft Library, University of California, Courtesy Lenore Glen Offord

Middle-aged Cordelia Botkin won a younger man away from his wife and, when jilted, sent her a savage box of sweets.

Cordelia Botkin's rare power as a charmer is hard to explain. She was stocky in figure and heavy of face, with a drooping mouth and fatty chin. Her eyes may have been the reason—they were dark and deep. In 1895, the year she becomes of interest, Cordelia was a dumpy San Francisco matron of 41. Married but separated from Welcome A. Botkin, she had a precocious son named Beverly who in his teens had already embraced the vices of a grown man.

One of Cordelia's simple pleasures was to sit in quiet contemplation on a bench in a park near her home. Bicycle riding was the sport for men in those days, and fast bike riders were called Scorchers. Cordelia much enjoyed watching the Scorchers race by. One day a real Scorcher alighted near her to fix his bicycle. He was John Presley Dunning, manager of the local branch of the Associated Press, whose career as a noted war correspondent had been tarnished by addiction to slow horses and fast women. Handsome, spoiled, self-indulgent, Dunning was fully a decade younger than Cordelia. Yet the two began talking and—incredibly!—he succumbed to her charm.

Dunning had a wife who was the daughter of Rep. Penington, U.S. Congressman from Dover, Delaware. The couple had a small child. On meeting Cordelia, Dunning dropped all pretense of living with his family. He moved with Cordelia, the charmer, into an apartment at 927 Geary Street. Here they were joined by Cordelia's son and his newest paramour, a woman his mother's age. The ménage rang to continuous revelry, with so much bottle-smashing and laughter that neighbors complained.

Up to now Mrs. John Dunning had been long-suffering about her husband. But his infatuation for homely Cordelia proved too much to bear. In 1896, she returned with her child to Dover, where she began receiving a series of anonymous letters. Postmarked San Francisco, the first of the letters contained the news that her husband was living in sin with a pretty English woman. It was Cordelia's quaint conceit that she was both English and pretty, and when Dunning finally read the unsigned letters he unhesitatingly called her the author.

Cordelia's bliss ended two years later, with the Spanish-American War, when Dunning was ordered by the AP to cover the fighting in Cuba. On leaving, he broke the news that he had no plans for returning. She tried to follow him as a front-line nurse, but her application was turned down. She brooded, moving restlessly around San Francisco. One day she found a way to occupy her mind. . . .

John Presley Dunning, talented newspaperman, lived a fast life with Cordelia until he was dispatched to cover the Spanish-American War.

The scene shifts to the Penington porch in quiet Delaware. On the mellow evening of August 9, 1898, Rep. Penington sat surrounded by his daughters and grandchildren. They had just finished a six o'clock dinner of fresh-caught trout and corn fritters. A nephew had taken a stroll by the post office and now he returned bearing a package, postmarked San Francisco, for Mrs. Dunning. She stripped off the outer wrapping. Inside was a pink oblong box with the word "Bonbons" embossed gaily on the cover. This was tied with a pink ribbon, its elegance in contrast to a piece of paper torn from a cheap pad which bore the written message "With love to yourself and baby, Mrs. C." Under this lay a cambric handkerchief, its twenty-five-cent price tag still visible. Uncovered, the candy in the box looked clumsily homemade.

Mrs. Dunning and her sister ate several large pieces, commenting on the gritty lumps inside. Rep. Penington kept to his evening chew of tobacco, but the children took small bites. Next day Mrs. Dunning and her sister were violently ill, the children less so. On August 12th, the two women were dead. By then, the candy had been analyzed and found to be injected with arsenic. The handwriting on the package resembled that of the anonymous letters. Summoned home, Dunning identified the letters as Cordelia's.

Even so, the case against Cordelia Botkin was weak, for she had not been seen buying or mailing the candy. The only concrete evidence against her came from a druggist who had sold her powdered arsenic, which she told him was for cleaning a straw hat. Yet the arsenic in the candy was partly crystalline! Next came the knotty question of whether she could be tried in San Francisco for a crime committed in far-off Delaware. The Governor of California pondered a long time before deciding the trial should be held in his state.

Cordelia, meanwhile, was busy denying all, claiming that an unknown enemy had set out to wrong her. She felt encouraged on learning that fingerprint evidence was not allowed in California courts. Yet other things worked against her. Spectators at the trial thought her own lawyers acted as if she were guilty. Dunning, arriving from Delaware, was rude. On the witness stand, he stated loudly, "This is more of a duty than a pleasure."

Now, if ever, Cordelia needed her uncanny ability to charm. But at this crucial moment, she failed with the twelve men of the jury, who gave her life imprisonment. Behind bars, however, the charm snapped back. She became the pet of the prison, allowed many unusual privileges, including frequent shopping trips to town. On one of these she found herself sitting in a trolley opposite the judge who tried her. She smiled, he glared. The San Francisco earthquake of 1906 ended this lush life. Because of it, Cordelia was transferred to San Quentin. There, an ordinary prisoner, she died in 1910.

The petite Mrs. Dunning died from dipping into the box of chocolates sent from San Francisco to Delaware.

56

16. THE GIRL IN ROOM 84

The bludgeon which smashed in the skull of pretty Emmeline "Dolly" Reynolds was an ugly instrument to behold.

It looked like a sawed-off walking cane or shepherd's crook. It was lethal—14½ inches of iron pipe, with another ⅜-inch iron driven through the center as a death-dealing core. The straight end was wrapped tight with a heavy mound of lineman's tape. The crook had been made by driving a cold chisel deep into the metal, bending the pipe over the cut.

This gruesome iron club struck Dolly in the early hours of August 16, 1898, the year that the nation was engrossed in the Spanish-American War. Dolly was hit in Room 84 of the Grand Hotel, at Broadway and 31st Street, in New York City. She had registered at noon the day before, writing in the register *E. Maxwell and wife, Brooklyn.* The hotel staff watched her as she did this, for Dolly was young, stylish, and very pretty. Late in the afternoon a man joined her and a festive bottle of champagne was dispatched to Room 84. That evening the two stepped out, Dolly aglitter like a jewelry store. Presumably they went uptown to dinner and a show. At 11:30 P.M. they were back at the hotel. At 2:30 A.M., the man left, acting furtive.

A maid found Dolly's lifeless body the next morning, lying in the traditional pool of blood. Beside her lay the bludgeon, its taped end clotted with blood and Dolly's brains. The body was fully dressed, but the jewelry had been roughly yanked from her fingers and ears. Between Dolly's corset and the cold flesh, police discovered a check for $13,000. This bore the bold signature of Dudley Gideon and seemed a highly promising clue. But no one ever located a Dudley Gideon and in time he was branded a phony. On the back of the check was an endorsement by S. J. Kennedy. Here police were luckier. A dentist of that name had an office on West 22nd Street.

Dolly was identified by papers in her handbag. Detectives tracking back on her short life discovered that she was close to being what the era called a sporting woman. She had left her well-off family in Mount Vernon when in her teens, to live her own life in the big city. Shortly she met Maurice B. Mendham, prosperous broker. With no hesitation she allowed him to set her up in an apartment on West 58th Street. He lavished jewels on her and, when Dolly got a toothache, sent her to Dr. Samuel J. Kennedy.

The signature that Dolly Reynolds put in the hotel register never gave a clue to the identity of Maxwell or to her murderer.

Courtesy of The New York Historical Society

Police reasoned that Dolly and the dentist had been meeting clandestinely. This made Mendham a prime suspect since he could have discovered the erring couple and killed Dolly in a fit of jealous fury. But Mendham's perfect alibi placed him in New Jersey at the time of the murder. So the suspicions of the law swung to 31-year-old Dr. Kennedy. He vigorously denied ever seeing Dolly outside his office or endorsing

her check. His wife and children were out of town for the summer and on the night in question he had gone to Proctor's 23rd Street Theatre, where he slept through a noisy vaudeville show. Police found this hard to believe. They put him in the line-up and hotel employees picked him out. "We've got our man," the cops said.

But had they? Samuel J. Kennedy was an unassuming chap who lived in Staten Island with his own family and his parents. The parents swore he was home at 3 A.M. when they checked his bedroom. It would be impossible for him to leave the Grand Hotel at 2:30 A.M. and be home in half an hour. Other Staten Islanders told of seeing him on the midnight ferry. He was dozing, which bore out his story of sleepiness.

Police brushed this aside, producing a haberdasher near the Grand Hotel who recalled selling a hat on the afternoon before the murder. The customer had been talkative, confiding that he was a dentist named Kennedy. Police also advanced the novel theory that Kennedy had got to Room 84 with the bludgeon *inside* his trousers, hooked around the waistband or crotch. They assumed that, once in the room, he hid the weapon until time to kill Dolly.

Kennedy offered a blanket denial, and accused someone of impersonating him. The writing on the check was not his, he maintained, and at his trial experts bore this out. He had not bought a new hat, nor was he the type to tell his name to salesmen. Still, he was found guilty and condemned to death. With the Spanish-American War over, the trial dominated the news and New Yorkers began to ponder the verdict. Protests were heard, and a new trial ordered. At it the identification by hotel employees was less definite and the jury stood eleven to one for acquittal. A third jury also disagreed. Dr. Kennedy had now spent three years in jail and it seemed enough. He was released on bail and conveniently forgotten. . . .

A stylish coiffure gave Dolly the look of a debonair lady about town when in fact she was a suburban girl gone wrong.

Mystery writer Baynard Kendrick (using his fictional sleuth Duncan McClain) has turned his deductive powers on the Dolly Reynolds mystery. He believes someone *did* impersonate Kennedy. Maurice Mendham, he reasons, was weary of Dolly. Kendrick thinks Mendham persuaded a friend to dine and wine her, then pretend to buy her off for the sum of $13,000. But why forge Kennedy's name on the back of the check? Because inevitably an irate Dolly would wave the worthless check under Mendham's nose. Mendham would examine it, see Kennedy's name, and accuse the girl of infidelity. This would give him a neat excuse for terminating the love affair at no cost.

On the murder night a robbery was reported at the Grand Hotel. Kendrick thinks a burglar peered in on Dolly just after the man left. The $13,000 check might have been put in her bosom, but she still shone with diamonds and could have been counting $500 known to be in her pocketbook. The burglar might have climbed catlike through the window, stolen up behind her and lifted his terrible club.

Yet this only raises another question. The murder weapon was left in Dolly's room, and the New York *World* said of it, "The maker of the weapon seemed to take great pride in it." Would a hardened criminal leave such a cherished bludgeon behind? It seems unlikely . . .

Dolly's handbag contained papers that started the police on a futile search.

Dentist S. J. Kennedy vigorously denied an illicit romance with Dolly. He was such an unlikely lover-murderer that charges against him were finally dropped.

Courtesy of The New York Historical Society

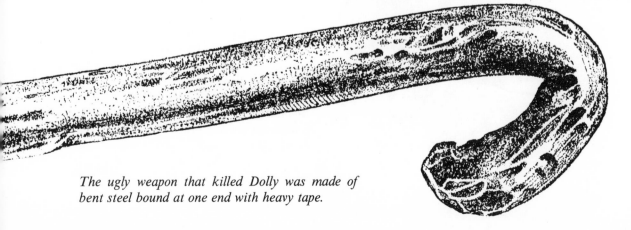

The ugly weapon that killed Dolly was made of bent steel bound at one end with heavy tape.

17. CURIOUS MEMBER OF A GENTLEMEN'S CLUB

Courtesy of The New York Historical Society

The exclusive Knickerbocker Athletic Club, 45th Street and Madison Avenue in New York, was an unlikely place for a fatal poisoning. The Knickerbocker was a dignified gentlemen's club. Many of the older members held important commands during the Civil War. Younger members, lifting dumbbells and playing squash, used the club gym to keep aristocratically fit.

Nothing less than a blue Bromo Seltzer bottle exploded the mystery of the Knickerbocker Club. It arrived by mail on Christmas Eve 1898, addressed to Harry Cornish, the Club's athletic director. Cornish, a jolly fellow, laughed long and loud, thinking a clever friend had sent him a safeguard against holiday indulgence. He left the bottle on his desk over Christmas Day, then carried it home to his boardinghouse, which was run by elderly Mrs. Katharine Adams. Three days later Mrs. Adams awoke with a splitting headache and for it allowed the sympathetic Cornish to fix her a Bromo. She drank it, complaining that the fizzy mixture tasted bitter. Cornish took a sip—to him it tasted all right. In a few seconds Mrs. Adams lay on the floor, in convulsions. Cornish, deathly ill from his sip, was barely able to summon help. In half an hour Mrs. Adams was dead. Cornish was taken to the Club, where he almost died.

Roland B. Molineux looked every inch the healthy gentleman athlete when he worked out at the Knickerbocker Club.

Now the Club doctor stepped center stage. A few months before he had attended a member named H. C. Barnet, resident of the Club. Barnet had died, apparently of diphtheria. Yet in his delirium the young man raved of a mysterious bottle which had arrived in the mail. The physician hastened to the Adams boardinghouse, where he found the Bromo Seltzer. Analyzed, it was found to be a harsh and terrible poison named cyanide of mercury.

Detectives swarmed over the Knickerbocker, ruining the club-chair slumber of older members. A murder in such surroundings seemed to demand the services of a Sherlock Holmes, but because Harry Cornish was careless, the break came quickly: the torn wrapper of the poison bottle still lay on top of his desk!

Club officials grabbed it to compare with handwriting in their files. It appeared to resemble the writing of Roland Molineux, son of Brigadier-General Molineux, one of the more distinguished Club members. Thirty-year-old Roland had been a member until recently, but had resigned after an argument with Harry Cornish. At a meeting of the executive committee, Roland issued the angry ultimatum, "Either Cornish is fired, or I resign." The committee slapped him in the face by voting to retain Cornish.

Yellow journalism still flourished and the *Journal* promptly named Molineux the poisoner.

The Knickerbocker Athletic Club, New York City, a stately spot for attempted murder.

Courtesy of The New York Historical Society

Harry Cornish, athletic director, aroused Molineux's particular hatred.

Other papers feared to go so far, but reported that police were working slowly toward an arrest. In late February, Molineux was at last taken into custody. Reporters described him as pleasant, jaunty, and handsome. He had a feline look, the feline he resembled being a tomcat for he had been named correspondent in a divorce case at the tender age of fifteen. Molineux had recently married a pretty girl named Blanche Cheeseborough. His rival for her dainty hand had been H. C. Barnet. Only after Barnet's death did the girl consent to marry Molineux.

Press and public indignation against Molineux ran high. At his trial five hundred men were questioned before an open-minded dozen could be found for a jury. The trial lasted three months, costing the State of New York $200,000. General Molineux, steadfastly at his son's side, reputedly spent more. Day by day a web of evidence coiled around the neck of the jaunty young man. He had been boss of a color factory in Newark, which gave him easy access to cyanide of mercury. Fourteen experts identified his handwriting as that on the Cornish package. The package had been mailed from the General Post Office at the hour Molineux usually arrived home from Newark. Prior to the killings he rented two mailboxes in the names of his victims. In Barnet's name he

61

Molineux sent away for patent medicines (ABOVE) in the name of his victims (LEFT).

The letters asked for harmless medicine, but Molineux emptied the bottles and re-filled them with poison.

sent for Kutnow's Stomach Powder, then refilled the bottle with poison. His lawyers were ingenious, but Molineux had no real case. In eight hours he was found guilty.

The Sing Sing Death House became his home for the following eighteen months. There he wrote a book of prison stories called *The Room with the Little Door.* On publication, critics hailed him as a talented writer. At length the Court of Appeal granted him a new trial, on the grounds that testimony about Barnet had been introduced in a trial involving Mrs. Adams and Cornish.

The second trial came in 1902. Time had obscured the details of the poisonings, indignation had flown, and Molineux seemed only a long-suffering man with literary talent and a pretty wife. In court, he was jovial and, in a record four minutes, the jury set him free.

In private life, he became a full-time writer, with David Belasco producing one of his plays. As a uniquely qualified expert, he was a feature-writer covering most of New York's subsequent murder trials. His wife divorced him and he married again. All of which earned him an entry in Who's Who, where his years 1898–1902 were discreetly described as "Out of employment."

Yet in Roland Molineux were the seeds of insanity. In 1913, he was committed to the King's Park Hospital for the Insane. He died there four years later.

President William McKinley enjoyed his visit to the Pan-American Exposition in Buffalo. Weather was fine and large crowds roared welcome. Guards relaxed, feeling no one would harm so contented a man.

1901

18. THE PRESIDENT
NO ONE WOULD HARM

At 4 P.M. the big doors opened wide and the crowd shoved in to proceed—first in double, then in single file—along the sixty-four foot aisle which would put each in position to shake hands with William McKinley, twenty-fifth President of the United States. . . .

It was September 6, 1901, at the Pan-American Exposition in Buffalo. There was no tension, only pleasure, in the sunny air that day and few seemed more content than the President. One thing the amiable McKinley dearly loved was shaking hands with the electorate. He was a whiz at it, having perfected a fast-grip technique which permitted him to shake fifty hands a minute.

Today he had offered to shake hands for fifteen minutes in the Temple of Music, an ornate building built for the rousing band music of John Philip Sousa. September 5th, the day before, had been President's Day at the beautiful Exposition with its lagoons and gardens. McKinley had spoken (without loudspeakers!) to fifty thousand enthusiastic listeners. On the morning of the 6th, he visited Niagara Falls, carefully going no farther than the halfway point of the International Bridge, for at that time no American President had set foot outside the United States.

One aide thought the President had pressed his luck far enough by addressing fifty thousand

63

The young man approaching McKinley in a line of handshakers seemed to have an injured right hand, but under the bandage was a revolver. When the President reached for his left hand the assassin pulled the trigger.

people the day before and mingling with crowds at the Falls this morning. He urged McKinley to cancel the Temple of Music handshaking. "Why should I?" the President asked. "No one would wish to hurt me." This was unanswerable. President William McKinley was not a man who aroused passion.

At 4 o'clock that afternoon, he stationed himself before a bower of potted bay and palm trees, festooned with American flags. It was halfway down the main aisle of the Temple, allowing those who had shaken hands to depart swiftly by a side door. Near the stage an organ softly played a Bach Sonata. In all some fifty various guards protected the Chief Executive. Twelve uniformed Exposition guards stood at the Temple Entrance. Inside eighteen others, plus eleven soldiers, formed two lines along the lane through which the handshakers passed. All the guards had strict orders to intercept anyone whose behavior looked suspicious. Close to the President stood four Buffalo detectives, one of them directly behind him. Facing McKinley, three feet away (behind the

handshakers), were two Secret Service men. A third was ten feet away. Four more soldiers stood beside the two aides on both sides of McKinley.

The portly President, attired in a frock coat and white linen vest, seemed the only cool person in the muggy auditorium. As the crowd poured in, handkerchiefs were much in evidence mopping brows. One man, wearing the flannel shirt of a workingman, took out his handkerchief and seemed to wrap it around his right hand, as if protecting an injury. This was a suspicious gesture but no guard noted it. One reason was the man's face, later described as blankly innocent. "He was the last man in the crowd we would have picked out as dangerous," an officer said.

The man with the handkerchief around his hand was Leon Czolgosz (pronounced *Cholgosh*). He was 28, the son of immigrant parents who had settled in the Midwest. Poorly educated, he worked in factories and had developed a grievance against all those better off. He tried to ally himself with Anarchists, who would have none of him. A year before he read with excitement of

McKinley was treated ineptly by doctors and slowly died. "It is God's way—His will be done," he told his wife. His successor, Theodore Roosevelt, gave Secret Service full responsibility for protecting Presidents.

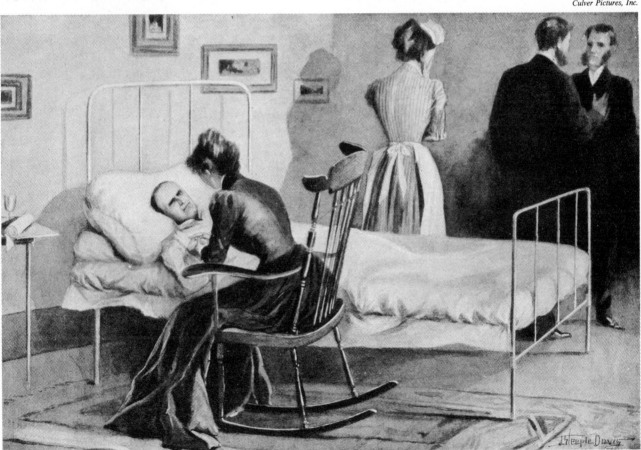

a New Jersey workingman who traveled to Italy to kill King Humbert. As Czolgosz said later, he thought, "It would be a good thing for this country to kill the President."

The object under Czolgosz' handkerchief was a .32 caliber Iver Johnson revolver. At 4:07 P.M. the young man faced McKinley, who affably reached for his left hand since the right seemed injured. Czolgosz brushed the hand aside and lunged, firing twice. One bullet hit a button and bounced off, the other entered the left side of McKinley's abdomen, penetrating front and rear walls. McKinley stiffened for a moment, looking at Czolgosz in hurt astonishment. Between them the handkerchief flared, set afire by the shot. Guards and soldiers pounced on the assassin, who muttered, "I done my duty." One guard took careful aim and punched Czolgosz in the nose. "Be easy with him, boys," the President called weakly.

Eight days later McKinley was dead of gangrene of the pancreas. In retrospect the doctors seem to have bungled, but at the time few thought so. The country cried out for Czolgosz's blood. Only seventeen days after the assassination he was placed on trial, with two reluctant defense lawyers appointed by the court two days before. Czolgosz was no flamboyant figure like Guiteau. He remained cryptic, expressing his silent contempt for the American judicial system. In two sessions of four hours each, he was found guilty and sentenced to death. On October 29th, he was electrocuted in Auburn Prison. "I am not sorry," he said, as the straps tightened.

Between 1865 and 1901, three Presidents of the United States had been killed by assassins. "Our record is appalling," thundered Judge Colt, of the United States Circuit Court. "We are worse than any European country." He echoed national sentiment, and Theodore Roosevelt, the new President, ordered the U.S. Secret Service to assume total responsibility for the protection of future Chief Executives.

66

As prison authorities and official witnesses watched, Czolgosz was executed two months after killing President McKinley. The first electrocution in the U.S. occurred at the same Auburn Prison in 1890.

19. ANDREW CARNEGIE'S "DAUGHTER"

Brown Brothers

Andrew Carnegie, richest man in the land, was so forbidding that no one dared ask if he had an illegitimate daughter.

On a bright day in the late Nineties, Mrs. Leroy Chadwick of Ohio—"Cassie" to friends—took a trip to New York. The wife of a socially prominent Clevelander who was also an unsuccessful physician, Cassie Chadwick was a vivid female with bright green eyes and stunning auburn hair. She was well into her thirties, a matronly bulk obscuring what had once been the bloom of beautiful youth.

In New York, the lady engaged a suite at the Holland House, a hotel favored by wealthy Ohioans. In the lobby she bumped into a Cleveland lawyer named Dillon and begged him to accompany her on a personal errand. To Dillon's amazement, the carriage stopped before the magnificent Fifth Avenue residence of Andrew Carnegie, America's richest man. Cassie asked the lawyer to wait, and tripped to the front door of the block-size mansion. Using her full personality, she talked her way past butler and footmen to the presence of the Carnegie housekeeper. Informing this personage that she planned to hire a maid who had been in the Carnegie employ, she asked an estimate of the girl's honesty and

Cassie Chadwick of Cleveland tripped into this impressive Fifth Avenue mansion to begin America's most amazing swindle.

Brown Brothers

ability. The housekeeper answered that no such maid had ever worked there. Cassie expressed surprise, then deliberately went on to prolong the conversation as long as possible. Twenty minutes later, waving a friendly goodbye to the butler, she departed the mansion. Getting into the carriage she stumbled slightly, dropping a paper. Gallant lawyer Dillon retrieved it—and noticed it was a promissory note for $2,000,000 signed by Andrew Carnegie!

So began the most brazen swindle in American history. For now, assuming a caught-at-last air, Cassie batted eyelashes over green eyes and confessed that she was Andrew Carnegie's illegitimate daughter. All the world knew the Scotch-born millionaire had promised his mother never to marry while she lived, which made him an elderly bachelor who might indeed have a bastard child. As this flitted across Dillon's mind, Cassie went on to say that, as Carnegie's only offspring, she stood to inherit his huge fortune of $400,000,000. Meantime, the old man doted on her, and persisted in giving her money. This $2,000,000 note, for instance. Why, in a bureau drawer at home, she had another $7,000,000 in loose securities.

None of this was even remotely true. Cassie was born Liz Bigley, on a Canadian farm. A pretty girl with larceny in her veins, she ran away

United Press International Photo

to Toronto when in her teens. There she had calling cards printed which read MISS BIGLEY – HEIRESS TO $15,000. Department stores fell all over her, begging the nervy girl to take home showy wardrobes on account. She took several before skipping to the United States. There, in a mixture of extortion, blackmail, and prostitution she averaged $1,000 a week from men met in Pullman cars. By the time she met Dr. Chadwick, Cassie had served a three-year prison term for fraud. The two met in a bordello, where Cassie convinced the simple-minded doctor she dwelled only to teach the girls good manners and cleanliness. On becoming the social Mrs. Leroy Chadwick, she began an intensive study of Andrew Carnegie's life and habits. During long hours, she practiced forging his signature. She was setting up the country's wealthiest man for the Big Con.

Cassie had also picked lawyer Dillon with care, for she needed a type who on Fifth Avenue would swear to keep her secret forever, at home would promptly tell. Dillon got back to Cleveland first and, when Cassie returned, social and banking circles were abuzz with the story of her fortunate illegitimacy. Dillon urged her to take a safe-deposit box for the $7,000,000 in her drawer. On his recommendation, she carried an envelope to a banker who, without examining the contents, unhesitatingly handed her a receipt for $7,000,000. With this receipt, her ability to forge Carnegie's signature, and the story of her illegitimacy, Cassie now commanded untold amounts of money.

She figured that Carnegie was such a terrifying man nobody would dare ask him if he had an illegitimate child. In this, she was one-hundred-percent correct. She had also figured other angles. By apparently keeping $7,000,000 in a drawer, she neatly planted the idea that she herself might be played for a sucker. Swallowing this bait, bankers and businessmen in Ohio and elsewhere sought the privilege of loaning her large sums of money. They did so at exorbitant interest rates, thinking Cassie was too simple to catch on. But Cassie had figured this, too. Pretending to be a sucker protected her further, since the banks would not dare reveal the loans because of the criminally high interest.

Cassie Chadwick, once pretty, was prematurely aged by the strains of her colossal hoax. Much of her money was spent on elaborate attire.

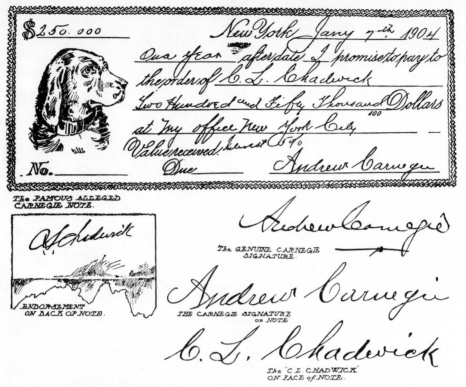

Cassie spent months practicing Carnegie's signature, never got it quite right. Yet she was able to get away with forged notes like the above. Under it, Carnegie's true signature; (MIDDLE) *Cassie's forgery;* (BOTTOM), *Cassie's own hand.*

"Deed of Trust" for $10,246,000 Signed with Carnegie's Name.

This is one of the "assets" of Mrs. Cassie L. Chadwick, a deed of trust for $10,246,000, signed with Andrew Carnegie's name:

Know all men by these presents that I, Andrew Carnegie, of New York City, N. Y., do hereby acknowledge that I hold in trust for Mrs. Cassie L. Chadwick, wife of Dr. Leroy S. Chadwick, of No. 1824 Euclid avenue, city of Cleveland, county of Cuyahoga, and State of Ohio, properly assigned and delivered to me for said Cassie L. Chadwick by her uncle, Frederick R. Mason in his lifetime (now deceased), which property is of the appraised value of ten millon, two hundred and forty-six thousand dollars ($10,246,000), consisting of 2,500 shares of Great Western Railway stock of England and Wales, valued at two million, one hundred thousand dollars ($2,100,000); 1,800 shares of Caledonian Railway stock of Scotland, valued at one million, one hundred and forty-six thousand dollars ($1,146,000), and bonds of the United States Steel Corporation of New Jersey bearing five per cent. interest of the par value of seven million ($7,000,000) dollars.

The income from the above described property I agree to pay over to said Cassie L. Chadwick semi-annually between the first and fifteenth days of June and December of each year during the life of this trust, without any deduction or charges for services or expenses of any kind, this trust to be and remain in full force until Aug. 29, 1902.

In case of the death of said Andrew Carnegie, said trust to terminate immediately and said property income and all proceeds to vest absolutely both in law and equiey in said Cassie L. Chadwick; in case of the death of Cassie L. Chadwick, said trust to terminate immediately and all of said property, together with all income and proceeds thereof, to be transferred and turned over to the heirs-at-law of legal representations of said Cassie L. Chadwick.

I further agree to faitfully carry out all of the above provisions and that all of said stocks and bonds have been indorsed over in the name of said Cassie L. Chadwick, so that no further or other act will be necessary on my part or on the part of my legal representatives to put said Cassie L. Chadwick or her heirs-at-law in full possession of same on the termination of ths trust.

Witness my hand and seal this 27th day of February, 1901   ANDREW CARNEGIE.

Cassie used Carnegie's name in a multitude of ways. (ABOVE), *text of a Deed of Trust for no less than $10,246,000. Supposedly signed by Carnegie, it brought Cassie added millions.*

70

Cassie borrowed from one and all. Incredible as it may seem, she took in over $1,000,000 a year and spent it on $100,000 dinner parties, $90,000 necklaces, and grand pianos for friends. She installed a pipe organ in her Cleveland home for the edification of Dr. Chadwick, who believed he could play. Yet Cassie only wanted money to spend it. She was a compulsive spender who got her thrills from watching the money disappear.

For seven years the mad whirl continued, with banks allowing the loans to ride while interest accrued, expecting to cash in gloriously when Carnegie died. But inevitably Cassie got a bad break. It came in November 1904, after she had borrowed $190,000 from a Boston bank. For once, the bank demanded its money back on time. Cassie didn't have it and the bank sued. The story reached the newspapers and her bubble burst. In Oberlin, Ohio, the bank president admitted loaning $800,000 to Cassie. The admission began a run on the bank, for which she was blamed. Now, at last, someone had to speak to Andrew Carnegie, who issued a death-blow statement: "Mr. Carnegie does not know Mrs. Chadwick of Cleveland. Mr. Carnegie has not signed a note for more than thirty years."

Banks failed, firms toppled. Newspapers estimated Cassie had swindled ten to twenty million dollars. It was impossible to tell how much for many bankers, fearing to expose their gullibility, covered up losses in mysterious ways. Cassie was in New York when exposure came, living in an entire floor of the Holland House which she rented by the year. As she moved about town, trying to explain to bankers, crowds clogged the streets for sight of her. Taken back to Cleveland, she was a broken woman. At her trial she pleaded guilty—what else could she do?—and the jury sentenced her to ten years. Jailhouse life was far different from Holland House life and Cassie withered. One night in 1907, she rolled over on the hard iron cot and died.

Cassie's bubble finally burst. Here she shakes hands with a juvenile well-wisher as she leaves New York in custody for Cleveland. There, the entire police force held back the curious.

71

Nan Patterson, second from right, was a replacement in the famed Florodora Sextette. Most Florodora girls wed millionaires. Nan fell for a married gambler.

20. THE GIRL IN THE HANSOM CAB

At the turn of the century, New York's Great White Way was a dazzling place for those who could afford its gay, fun-filled life. To the married man of wealth, the era also offered a convenient double-standard which let him stay out late while his wife uncomplainingly remained home. If he turned his eyes toward the bright lights of Broadway, he found frivolous girls of the theater and elsewhere eager to barter their virtue for a bird-and-bottle midnight supper at Rector's.

In 1904, the first of two ultra sensational murders glued the eyes of the nation to the Great White Way. The central figure in the first case was a doll-faced girl named Nan Patterson, just twenty years old at the time. Nan came of a good family, her father being supervising architect of the U.S. Treasury. She had made a runaway marriage in her teens, and been divorced soon after. She next won the considerable distinction of becoming a Florodora Girl. Not one of the original Sextette, to be sure, but a replacement for a

"With his left shoulder pressing me and his cheek almost touching mine he fumbled about for a minute. Suddenly his right hand came around with a jerk and touched my breast sharply. At that very instant the cab jolted and I heard a little muffled noise—nothing the least resembling the sharp crack of a pistol; I never dreamed of such a thing. The next instant he began to lean more heavily against me, and then—his head rolled into my lap. I put my hand on his cheek--IT WAS GROWING COLD!"

Nan's version of how Caesar Young met his death: in the hansom cab, she sat by in mute amazement as he shot himself over leaving her.

State's version had Nan pulling gun. When Caesar grabbed it, she instinctively pulled the trigger.

THE WORLD: SATURDAY EVENING, NOVEMBER 26, 1904.
THE GENERALLY CREDITED IDEA OF HOW CAESAR YOUNG CAME TO HIS DEATH.

"tell-me-pretty-maiden" girl who departed the cast to marry.

Many of the Florodora girls married millionaires, but it was Nan's destiny to fall in love with a gambling man. Caesar Young had been a popular amateur athlete in his native England. In America, the handsome, breezy fellow discovered an uncanny ability to bet on winning horses. Beginning as a race-track gambler he had achieved the high status of bookmaker and horse breeder. Along each step of the way he had been assisted by an astute, quick-minded wife. When he met Nan Patterson in 1902 Caesar had been married for ten years.

Immediately the showy pair fell in love and became fixtures in the sporting world, seen at the races and gambling spas, in expensive restaurants and plush hotels. Yet Caesar Young had headaches. He still needed his wife, whose sharp mind made his bookmaking and horse breeding possible. At the same time, Nan's endearing young charms had a grip on him. For two years Caesar shuttled between wife and mistress-who-wanted-to-be-wife. In New York, he kept Mrs. Young in one hotel and Nan in another on the same block. This enabled him to pass days with his wife and nights with Nan. Even so, the pressures got him. He tried to persuade Nan to take a trip to Europe, but she flatly refused. He then made reservations for himself and Mrs. Young on the *Germanic*, sailing at the early hour of 9:30 A.M. on June 4, 1904.

As sailing day neared, Nan made greater efforts to get Caesar to promise to marry her. Once she claimed to be four months pregnant, but Young would not buy this. He was a heavy drinker and, despite her glowing youth, Nan could keep up with him. On the night before sailing came a tense scene. Both were drunk, with Nan resuming pleas that he get a divorce. Caesar slapped her hard across the mouth and called her a dirty name. Then he contemptuously tossed a $100 bill in her lap. Nan may have been drunk, but she was sober enough to tuck the money in her stocking top.

"I never want to see you again, you —" Caesar snarled on parting that night. But he was up with

Courtesy of The New York Historical Society

74

ASST DISTRICT ATTORNEY
RAND CROSSEXAMINING
NAN PATTERSON

Through two headlined trials, Nan clung to her story—a difficult feat for a frivolous young girl. Here, Assistant D.A. Rand hammers questions at her.

the dawn, calling Nan on the phone. He told her to meet him at Columbus Circle, then he went to a bar for a brandy-and-whiskey breakfast. Nan arrived, also unfed, attired in a violet walking suit, with lavender-violet hat topped by red roses. They had several drinks together, then stepped into a hansom cab for a ride down Broadway to the *Germanic's* pier. En route, they stopped at two more bars. At West Broadway and Franklin Street, about halfway to the pier, passers-by heard an explosion in the cab. Those who rushed to the hansom found Caesar sprawled across Nan's lap, dying of a bullet wound in the chest. No gun was visible, though later one was found in his pocket. "Caesar, Caesar, why did you do this?" Nan was crying hysterically.

At the police station, Nan swore Caesar had shot himself in agony over leaving her. This was hard to believe, especially as only a contortionist could have shot a bullet into himself at the angle Caesar's entered. There was also the fact that, after shooting himself, a dying man would hardly place the gun carefully back in his pocket. Yet Nan stuck to her story through rigorous interrogation. Indeed, she never changed one syllable through two sensational trials. By her side at each trial sat her bewhiskered father, who brought great dignity to the proceedings. Pictures and sketches make Nan look plain, but in the flesh she was a personality kid. People instinctively liked her cheery ways and gay femininity, and two juries could not visualize the winsome girl with a smoking revolver in her hand. Nor could they go so far as to acquit her. After a second split jury, the State gave up, setting Nan free. For nearly a year she had been in jail, dreaming of her beloved bright lights. On her first night of freedom, Nan celebrated by getting gloriously drunk.

Now the girl was in a fine position to capitalize on her notoriety by starring in musical shows. She tried it but found that she had absolutely no talent. At this bleak moment in life, the husband of her girlhood marriage reappeared to pay new court to her. The two married again and soon separated. With this, the world loses track of the Girl in the Hansom Cab.

21. THE CRIME OF THE CENTURY

SCENE: New York's most picturesque building.
VICTIM: America's best known architect.
MURDERER: A millionaire playboy whose name made headlines.
CAUSE: A girl whose rare beauty adorned magazine covers and musical shows.

Out of this provocative potpourri exploded a crime which rocked the nation in 1906. Even at that date it was dubbed the Crime of the Century, and as such it has stood the test of time. Indeed, it might almost be called an educational crime, since it introduced the newspaper-reading public to many heretofore unknown aspects of sex behavior. Possibly it even prepared the country for the teachings of Dr. Freud. From the White House, President Theodore Roosevelt called the testimony "filth," and urged newspapers to cease printing it, but editors continued to print and the public continued to read. Admirers of pure mystery are inclined to disparage the case as lacking in suspense and subtlety. But the murder of Stanford White by Harry K. Thaw has

The Century's most celebrated murder was committed on Madison Square Garden Roof. Privileged guests were allowed to sit near the footlights. Stanford White occupied such a celebrity table when shot by Harry Thaw.

76

White, famous architect, designed the Garden and fifty other New York landmarks. By night, he enjoyed the high life of Great White Way.

never been equaled for widespread shock-interest and public fascination.

The spectacular murder took place on the Roof of the Madison Square Garden. Red-haired, beefy, dynamic Stanford White, 53, was the architect who had designed this picturesque terra cotta building at Madison Avenue and 26th Street, opposite the northeastern corner of Madison Square Park. In addition to the Garden, with its handsome Tower modeled after the Giralda in Seville, he was represented around New York City by some fifty other noted buildings and monuments, among them the Washington Square Arch.

Harry Kendall Thaw was a different breed. The scapegrace son of a Pittsburgh railroad and coke family, he was 34 years old, with a bland,

characterless face that sliced ten years from his age. Had Thaw been a poor man, he probably would have been in an asylum. As a member of a family that possessed millions, he was in constant hot water as a sadist who enjoyed whipping young girls and, some said, boys. An angry father had cut him off with a paltry $2,000 a year, but a doting mother quickly supplied him with an allowance of $80,000. Thaw peevishly complained that this was not enough.

The girl who drew these two together with such deadly force was Evelyn Nesbit, considered by many who saw her the loveliest looking girl who ever breathed. Evelyn could be innocent, she could be sultry, but however the girl looked she

The comely cause of the deadly conflict was Evelyn Nesbit, then the reigning beauty of New York. First White's protégée, she later wed Thaw.

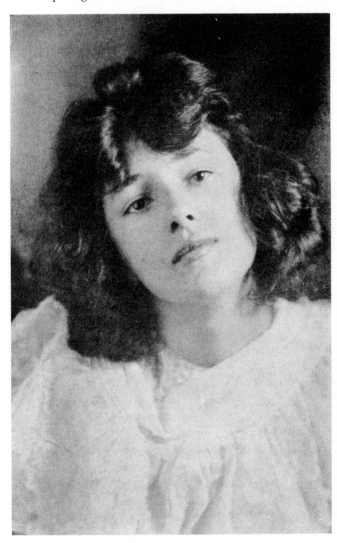

The scion of Pittsburgh millions, Thaw dined like a rich boy when imprisoned in New York City's Tombs. Expensive meals were sent from Delmonico's Restaurant, four miles uptown.

was breathtakingly beautiful. A top-artists' model and show girl at fifteen, she had been seduced by White in an elaborate hideaway where a red velvet swing billowed girl's skirts revealingly. Over the next few years Evelyn took money from the architect and was his radiant companion at midnight revels.

Enter Thaw who, on seeing Evelyn, desired her. Employing the family millions to top effect, he got her to accompany him to Europe. One night he whipped her so severely that she was confined to bed for two weeks. The pair next amazed the world by marrying. After the ceremony—Evelyn later testified—Thaw asked questions about her sex life. She described the seduction by White and this, her testimony said, aroused in Thaw an undying hatred—or was it total madness? He began calling White "The

Beast" or "The Bastard." Waving a revolver, he vowed to kill the architect to protect other young girls from Evelyn's fate.

On the night of June 25, 1906, the Thaws had seats for the opening of the new revue, *Mam'zelle Champagne* on the Madison Square Garden Roof. For the occasion Evelyn donned a daring white satin Directoire gown, topping it with a black picture hat. Harry wore a straw skimmer and a heavy winter overcoat, though it was summer. The two dined at Louis Martin's, just across the park from the Garden. Evelyn saw White at another table and slipped her husband a note, "That B is here." The couple then crossed the park and took an elevator to the Garden Roof. Shortly, White followed and was ushered alone to a table in the privileged section close to the footlights.

78

A model and a showgirl, Evelyn made a sultry gypsy in the pose above, demonstrating that she could use her beauty with skill.

Mam'zelle Champagne turned out to be dull and in time the Thaws rose to leave. As they passed an aisle Harry looked down its length and saw White framed dramatically at its end. His mind exploded. While the girls in the chorus chanted the words *I challenge you to a d-u-e-l,* he strode down the aisle and stopped before White, who pretended not to see him. Thaw waited a moment, then yanked out his pistol and fired three times into the architect's florid face.

Wrote Gerald Langford in 1962, "The trial can still be described as the most sensational ever held in an American court." Delphin Delmas, the Little Napoleon of the West Coast bar, had been imported as Thaw's chief counsel. Opposing him was the awesome William Travers Jerome, New York's vaunted D.A. At this peak moment of his career, Jerome was curiously inept, several times

losing his temper in court. Delmas, on the other hand, was wily. Evelyn, an experienced lady of twenty-two, appeared in court looking demurely innocent in sailor blouses and Buster Brown collars. A crowd of ten thousand milled outside as she parried Jerome's terrierlike examination. Inside the court spectators marveled at the aplomb with which she told the gamy details of her seduction.

The jury disagreed at the end of a long trial. At a second, Thaw was found not guilty by reason of insanity. This was a dubious triumph, for it meant confinement in a mental asylum. His mother immediately began using the Thaw millions to win Harry's release. For six years she kept at it, while Evelyn danced in vaudeville. When Thaw was released the couple was soon divorced. Harry was in and out of newspaper headlines until his death in 1936. Evelyn eventually found comfort in ceramics, living out a long life on the West Coast.

Evelyn's testimony was so shocking that she whispered details to D.A. William Travers Jerome.

22. AN AMERICAN TRAGEDY

Courtesy of Charles Boswell

Big Moose Lake in New York's Adirondacks, photographed at the time of Grace Brown's murder by Chester Gillette, had the remoteness and the camouflage needed for a forced drowning.

The crime of Chester Gillette, accused of slaying 18-year-old Grace Brown on July 11, 1906, forms the basis of Theodore Dreiser's monumental novel *An American Tragedy.*

In his book, Dreiser blamed a society which slowly grinds its victims down. But court records of the Chester Gillette case show a murderer driven by acute personal problems. Both Chester Gillette and Dreiser's Clyde Griffiths began at life's bottom. In the novel, Clyde is a weak, ambitious young man. In life, Chester Gillette seems to have been turned into a psychopath by callous neglect on the part of his parents.

Chester Gillette was the son of lay preachers, attached to the Salvation Army. More interested in saving souls than in the welfare of their son, these two carelessly parked Chester with friends and neighbors as they spread the gospel across the land. When Chester was fourteen his parents abandoned him altogether. Free as an orphan

he hit the road, making his way by a multitude of rough-and-tumble jobs, including that of railroad brakeman. (Dreiser's Clyde Griffiths, a onetime bellboy, is inexperienced by comparison.) Through all this Chester had an ace in the hole. A rich uncle operated the Gillette skirt (the novel changes this to *shirt*) factory in mid-state Cortland, New York. At last, when he was twenty, Chester wrote asking a job.

The uncle was not overly generous, offering a job as section foreman at a salary of $10 a week. Chester accepted and quickly discovered other rewards. As a nephew of the local factory owner, he was a conspicuous junior citizen of Cortland. Through the uncle's family he also had access to local society, with the strong possibility of marrying a wealthy girl. Chester, a cool, composed young man, knew this and had already begun showing interest in a girl he met socially. However, in his travels he had evolved a masterful seduction technique. With his life so well set, he still could not resist a detour in the direction of the prettiest girl working under him at the factory. She was 18-year-old Grace "Billy" Brown, tiny and bright, a farm girl moved to the city to earn $6 a week. Naïve Billy fell for worldly Chester and in the late spring of 1906 told him the bad news that she was pregnant. Having tasted the better things in life, 22-year-old Chester was determined not to let go of them. Still, the self-centered young man had to make some effort to cope with this sudden threat to his fine new world. He persuaded Billy to return to the farm, where he promised to join her in a few days. He didn't and during the weeks that followed she

Grace Brown, a $6.00 a week employee in the skirt factory where Chester was a foreman, became the victim of his philandering and then his warped emotions.

United Press International Photo

The nephew of the factory owner, Gillette showed his social aspirations in dapper attire such as this wing collar.

Courtesy of Charles Boswell

wrote him eight heart-rending letters. Billy Brown didn't ask marriage, but in the last letter she threatened to inform his uncle of her condition. This did the trick. Chester hastily asked for his vacation, borrowed $25, and went to meet Billy on July 8th.

The two spent that night in Utica, registered as man and wife. Next morning they took a train to the southern Adirondacks region of lakes and hills known as North Woods. After a night at Tupper Lake, they moved to Big Moose Lake, where Chester asked natives for "any old hotel where they have boats to rent." They were directed to the Glenmore Hotel. Here Chester signed a false name on the register, while Billy set down her right name and address.

July 11th was pleasantly hot, an ideal day for vacationists. The young couple breakfasted late, then ordered a picnic lunch which was placed in a suitcase. Renting a boat, they stowed the suitcase and a tennis racket aboard and rowed out on the large lake. What happened after that has engaged other minds besides Theodore Dreiser's, but nothing is known for certain except that at 7:45 P.M. Chester was seen hiking through the woods away from the lake, carrying the suitcase. He arrived alone at Eagle Bay, where he registered at the Arrowhead Hotel. After that he joined a happy group singing around a roaring fire.

Next day was fun and frolic for Chester Gillette. He passed it like any young man on vacation, sunning and flirting with girls. The day after he asked at the hotel if a drowning had been reported from Big Moose. "No," he was told. On July 14th the local law arrived to charge him with murder. Grace's body had floated to the surface, the face badly bruised. The coroner said she had died from blows, not drowning. A mound of new-turned moss on the shore revealed a buried tennis racket and Chester was accused of killing her with this. He denied it, offering a variety of stories. Once he said Billy had committed suicide by jumping overboard. Then he admitted that, while she could not swim, he could. Shrugging, he confessed he made no effort to rescue her.

Chester's father and mother were informed of his plight, but ignored him. His trial, lasting twenty-two days, was much publicized in the upstate press. Witnesses numbered 109, with so many from Cortland that the skirt factory had to be closed. From his cell, Chester sold photos of himself at $5 apiece and thus was able to afford meals from the local inn. Adorning the cell wall were pictures of pretty girls torn from magazines, one of them a cute trick who resembled Billy Brown. As with Theo Durrant, spectators found it hard to imagine such a calm, assured young man as a killer. However, the jury found him guilty on December 4th. He was electrocuted at Auburn on March 30, 1908, without confessing.

Chester's last stop with Grace, the Glenmore at Big Moose was a typical summer hotel of the region. It recently burned to the ground.

Mary Noonan McDonald (ABOVE) *was a lively lass who ran off with a priest. Husband Mike next wed Dora Feldman* (BELOW), *a burlesque queen. Mike was happy, but behind his back Dora carried on a December-May romance.*

Ill-fated with wives, Mike McDonald, was an awesome figure in Chicago politics and gambling. Edna Ferber used him as a character in Show Boat.

1907

23. MIKE McDONALD'S FAITHLESS BRIDES

Portly, powerful Michael Cassius "Mike" McDonald was fondly known in Chicago as The Big Boss and The King of the Gamblers. His success story was in the best Windy City tradition, for he had dealt himself upward from a small-time gambler on river boats to ownership of a thriving gambling establishment called The Store, at Clark and Monroe Streets.

Mike later served as the model for the gambling king in Edna Ferber's best-selling novel *Show Boat.* Yet gambling was only one of the man's activities. While still a gambler he branched out to become a ward heeler who could turn out a telling number of Democratic votes on Election Day. With increased prosperity, however, he began to consider gambling and ward-heeling beneath him. He kept his ownership of The Store and his connection with the Democrats, but tried to win respectability by founding a newspaper called the Chicago *Globe.* It failed

Webster Guerin, a high school student, was Dora Feldman McDonald's youthful foil. Despite pleas of his mother, Dora continued to pursue him.

United Press International Photo

84

MIKE M'DONALD'S YOUNG WIFE KILLS SORDID ADMIRER.

"He Blackmailed Me, but I Loved Him," She Cries, After Shooting Guerin in His Studio.

HER HUSBAND EX-KING OF CHICAGO GAMBLERS.

Under Mask of Courting Niece Artist Called on Millionaire's Wife for Years.

and Mike became a silent partner of Charles T. Yerkes, the multimillionaire traction king. He couldn't have made a smarter move. By the time he reached 70, Mike was several times a millionaire himself.

All of which should have bought him a contented old age. But it didn't, for Mike had terrible luck with the girls he married. The official explanation is that he spent so much time on the gambling-political-business side of his life that he left his wives home alone to invite temptation. But there must have been other reasons, for Mike's bad luck was truly phenomenal.

Mike's first wife died of natural causes. Trouble began when he married a vivacious Chicago beauty named Mary Noonan. One of Mary's first acts as Mrs. Mike was to get liquored up and shoot a cop who was making trouble in The Store. The cop died, but as a boss ward heeler, Mike easily hushed things up. Yet Mary Noonan McDonald had only begun. Soon she ran away with the popular minstrel man, Billy Arlington. An outraged Mike trailed the erring pair to the Palace Hotel in San Francisco. Mary jumped between singing Billy and Mike's avenging pistol, sobbing out, "Mike, for God's sake, don't shoot! It's all my fault! Take me back, for the love of God!"

Mike did, and built her a fine mansion on Ashland Avenue, close to the home of the Mayor.

Then he returned to his other activities. Mary had a private chapel in the Ashland Avenue house and she proceeded to set Chicago on its ear by running off with the priest who regularly came to hear her confession.

With this, Mike was fed up. He devoted himself to raising the children Mary left behind and stuck to a man's world populated by politicians, millionaires, and underworld figures. Still, a man needs some diversion and Mike preferred the lively art of burlesque. One night he watched a luscious, full-figured blonde on the stage. Her face, when finally his eyes reached it, looked familiar. Questioning elicited the fact that she was Dora Feldman, a girl who had grown up with his own children. Dora was married to a ballplayer named Sam Barclay, but the two were drifting apart. This gave Mike hope. He offered Barclay $30,000 to divorce Dora, and the ballplayer agreed. Dora made only one request. She asked Michael Cassius McDonald to embrace the Jewish faith, and he hastily converted from Catholicism.

So Dora, described at the time as an 18-kilowatt blonde, became the third Mrs. Mike. Her

The mansion that Mike built Dora was on Drexel Boulevard, as grand as the one he had built wife Mary.

husband was thirty-five years older than his bride, and she coyly called him Daddy. He built her a large mansion on Drexel Boulevard, then went back to business. The alliance lasted twelve long years, with Mike a happy, satisfied man. Yet behind his back trouble was brewing. In Dora, old Mike had been attracted to a girl in her twenties. She now evened the score by becoming enamored of a boy still in high school. He was Webster Guerin and by the time he was nineteen, the affair had reached such flaming proportions that his mother visited Dora, begging the blonde temptress to leave her boy alone. Dora tossed the lady out of the house.

Webster Guerin had artistic talent. After graduation he set himself up—no doubt with Dora's financial help—as a commercial artist in Room 703 of the Omaha Building at Van Buren and La Salle Streets. Time passed and he fell in love with a girl his own age. Dora went wild. The young couple ran away but Dora followed and pressured Webster into returning. Webster and the girl still saw each other; he still spent time with Dora. Finally, on the morning of February 21, 1907, Dora unexpectedly appeared in Webster's office. Angry argument was heard in the hall, followed by two sharp pistol shots. Those rushing in found Webster dead on the floor, shot through neck and heart. Smoking weapon in hand, Dora was on her knees beside him. "I loved him so much," she sobbed. At the police station, she pulled herself together to tell a chilling story of forcing Webster at pistol point to sit in a chair. "I told him I knew where his heart was and would not miss by an inch," she stated.

For Mike McDonald, it was the bitter end. Totally unaware of Dora's love affair, he took to his deathbed on hearing the details. To make a truly bizarre scene, Mary Noonan McDonald joined Dora (out on $50,000 bail) in fervent prayers beside the bed. Even so, Mike wasted away and died on August 9th.

Dora was now fortified by all Mike's millions. She hired the experienced Asa Trude as one lawyer and James Hamilton Lewis, newly elected U.S. Senator from Illinois, as another. In court, she used all her glittering wealth to add emphasis to a witness-stand story of being driven momentarily insane when spurned by a young lover. Senator Lewis' appeal to the jury has been called a masterpiece of legal pleading. Dora was found not guilty, but the jury was out six and a half tense hours before reaching the verdict.

24. "COME PREPARED TO STAY FOREVER"

Fire roared through the neat brick-and-frame farmhouse of Mrs. Belle Gunness, just a mile outside the pleasant town of La Porte, Ind., on the night of April 28, 1908.

At first, the fire seemed no more than a grim tragedy which took the lives of the widow Gunness and her three attractive children, aged eleven, nine, and five. Then questions began popping up. In life, 48-year-old Belle Gunness had stood 5'5", weighed a tremendous 280 pounds. Yet the body in the ruins weighed no more than 150. Had the inferno-like flames shriveled the mountain of flesh that was Mrs. Gunness? No one could be sure, since the head of the body was oddly missing. So another question arose. Had the head been severed by a falling beam—or been cut off by a murderer who set the fire to hide his crime?

Sheriff Smutzer of La Porte, arriving on the scene in a red Ford runabout, had few doubts. To him it was an open-and-shut case of murder plus arson. He set two deputies digging in the smoking debris for Belle's head, then issued orders for the immediate arrest of wispy, slow-witted Ray Lamphere, who had been Belle's daytime hired man and nighttime lover.

In his cups, Ray had boasted of nights spent with his employer, but La Porte had other evidence that a come-hither look lay in the depths of the outsize woman's china blue eyes. Burly Belle liked to dress in a man's rough overalls to do her own hog butchering. But on Sundays she got herself laced into a wasp-waist corset and drove off to church, often in the company of a stranger who had arrived with his suitcase at the railroad station a few days before. Ray Lamphere had endured a succession of these attentive strangers, but not until last winter had he lost his temper over one. Then Belle began introducing Andrew Helgelien, newly arrived from South Dakota, as her husband-to-be. Ray protested, and Belle fired him. The discarded lover began to drink and made attempts to force himself back on Belle, who had him arrested for trespassing. "I'm afraid he'll set fire to the place," she said meaningfully to the sheriff.

Locked up and charged with Belle's murder, Ray Lamphere shrilly protested innocence. As he did, Asle Helgelien showed up from South Dakota, in search of his brother Andrew. He told Sheriff Smutzer that Andrew had answered a matrimonial ad placed by Belle Gunness in a Norwegian-language newspaper. In her reply, Belle offered true love and a life of wedded bliss, but mentioned the need of a fast $1,000 to pay off a mortgage. She also revealed a strong prose style. "My heart beats in wild rapture for you, come prepared to stay forever," she urged An-

Belle Gunness seemed more the sturdy mother posing with her children than a sadistic lurer of lonely men.

Photo by N. E. Koch, Courtesy Lillian de la Torre

86

In the flesh Belle weighed an overwhelming 280 pounds, this dime-novel account of her exploits slims her do attractively. When Belle approached a man sleeping in spare room she had either love in her eye or poison in her ha

Courtesy Lillian de la T

The Mrs Guinness Mystery

A THRILLING TALE OF LOVE DUPLICITY & CRIME

Local officials looking through the remains of widow Gunness' burned-down house found eight men's watches, the first clues to Belle's fatal courtships.

drew. He did, after withdrawing his life savings from the bank. He was never heard from again.

Asle Helgelien was intuitive, positive his brother had met foul play. He felt more convinced when the men digging for Belle's head found eight men's watches in the rubble, together with assorted bones and human teeth. Asle also heard the details of the death of Peter Gunness, Belle's late husband. Belle said Peter had been killed when a meat grinder toppled from a shelf to crown him, but on seeing the body the coroner had muttered, "This is a case of murder!" One of Belle's children told a schoolmate, "My momma killed my poppa; she hit him with a cleaver." But at the inquest, Belle was so convincing and formidable that nothing was done.

Asle Helgelien wandered the Gunness acres, letting intuition run free. Belle had a hog pen, surrounded by a six-foot fence. In one corner was a rubbish hole. Asle shouted to the men digging in the ground. "Try here," he ordered. They did, and uncovered four bodies, skilfully sliced apart and wrapped in oilcloth. One body was Andrew Helgelien. Next day, three more bodies were turned up and, in all, fourteen of Belle's victims were pieced together, with a quantity of teeth, bones, and watches left over. The gruesome discoveries were headlined in Midwest newspapers and relatives appeared to claim bodies. All told the same story of lonesome men answering Belle's matrimonial ads which warned "Triflers need not apply," then hopefully traveling to La Porte with life savings in pockets. Sheriff Smutzer estimated that Belle had made $30,000 from her victims. She had drugged the suitors, smashed their heads, and dissected the bodies as she did her hogs.

The suitor who raised suspicions, Andrew Helgelien had come all the way from South Dakota in answer to one of Belle's matrimonial ads.

Ray Lamphere (RIGHT), Belle's jealous handyman, posed apprehensively with his lawyer in the trial that accused him of murdering the murderess.

Photo by N. E. Koch, Courtesy Lillian de la Torre

Crowds gaped as debris of the fatal fire was sluiced for Belle's teeth. First the teeth of the victims turned up. Finally Belle's bridge appeared, with a real tooth attached.

With this cleared up, the mystery of the body in the flames remained. Was it Belle's, or someone else placed there by the terrible Mrs. Gunness, a woman willing to kill her three children in the interests of a safe getaway? Belle's head never did appear but, the Sheriff reasoned, her false teeth might. A neighbor who had been a prospector back in '49 offered to sluice the debris for Belle's teeth. He found pages of books on anatomy and hypnotism, additional male teeth and watch parts. At last Belle's porcelain plates appeared, attached to an anchor tooth that was Belle's own.

This convinced many that the 150-pound body was Belle's. Others scoffed, saying a human monster like Old Woman Gunness would yank out one of her teeth in the interests of a safe escape. Controversy spilled over into the courtroom, for the sheriff doggedly insisted on bringing Ray Lamphere to trial as Belle's murderer. Both sides fought hard, and the jury brought in a curious verdict. Ray, who had contracted tuberculosis in jail, was acquitted of murder, but convicted of setting fire to the farmhouse. He got two to twenty-one years in the State pen.

Ray died in prison, after giving a rambling confession to a cell mate. He said he was aware of Belle's murder activities and had buried bodies for her. As to the headless woman in the fire, she was a female derelict imported by Belle from Chicago. Belle killed her with strychnine, put her in bed with the children, and set fire to the farmhouse. Belle had removed her own teeth, Ray said, then fled with the money brought her by the men who had expected happy matrimony.

Ray was supposed to hear from Belle after she got away safely. He never did, which leaves a final mystery: What happened to Belle?

25. THE THREE SISTERS IN BLACK

Three Sisters in Black, newspapers called them, for they had never been seen in anything but black dresses and coats, shroudlike scarfs, and heavy, dark veils. They traveled through Virginia, New York, Tennessee, and New Jersey, and in each spot neighbors grew outraged over what the grim trio did to forlorn Ocey Snead—a girl variously related as daughter, niece, and niece-daughter-in-law to the Three. Doctors who came to see an ailing Ocey said, in effect, "This girl is starving, all she needs is food." Explained one medical man, looking back, "The women were her blood relatives. I simply could not believe what my eyes told me."

Nor was the torture all physical. The frail girl detested the name Ocey, which stemmed from the way she mouthed her given name, Bessie, as a baby. The Three Sisters in Black knew she hated

Eccentric Virginia Wardlaw and her sisters dressed in funereal black and might have mourned over the fate of their own kin. (BELOW), *hard-eyed Virginia is led to jail.*

Mrs. Caroline Wardlaw Martin, mother of unhappy Ocey, and Mary Wardlaw Snead (BELOW) *made a dour pair in newspaper pictures.*

MOTHER AND AUNT OF THE BATHTUB VICTIM.

MRS. CAROLINE WARDLAW MARTIN.

the name Ocey. Yet they never ceased using it.

Protecting the weird Three Sisters was an immense gentility. They were Wardlaws, daughters of a Supreme Court Justice of South Carolina. Wardlaws had fought, bled, and died for the Confederacy. The three girls had been as close as triplets when young, but separated when one married a man named Snead and had two sons named John and Fletcher. The second married a true Confederate hero, Colonel Martin of the Kentucky Cavalry. Ocey was his daughter. This left Virginia Wardlaw, the brain of the family. She attended Wellesley and became a pioneer female educator. In 1900, she was appointed head of Montgomery Female College, at Christianburg, Virginia. Once she was settled there, the other two sisters abandoned their mates of many years to join her, bringing their children.

At first it was only the funereal attire of the Three Sisters that attracted attention. But then John Snead eloped with a Montgomery student. The Three Sisters pursued and brought young John back. Two days later cries of agony brought rescuers to the Wardlaw's campus home. John Snead lay writhing on the floor, clothing afire. In a short time he was dead—a suicide, mother and aunts wept. But grief was assuaged by an insurance policy for $12,000, recently taken out.

Local gossip called it murder, and the Three Sisters in Black decided to scatter. Mrs. Martin and Ocey, now about twelve, went to New York, where Colonel Martin joined them in a 57th Street boardinghouse. One night groans in the room caused the landlady to force the door. Inside, Ocey cowered on filthy rags in a corner, while Colonel Martin breathed weakly on the floor. Mrs. Martin regally surveyed the scene from the bed. Within minutes Colonel Martin was dead. His stricken widow solicited Confederate veterans in New York for funds to bury him. Only when he was underground did she recall a $10,000 policy taken out on her spouse.

Virginia Wardlaw had become head of Soule College, in Murfreesboro, Tennessee. The Sisters joined her in a huge, ghostly house furnished with a few iron cots. The black-clad three prowled the town day and night, earning a formidable reputation for eccentricity. Yet Virginia Wardlaw kept her job. Ocey, ever in bed, was said to be "sick." A doctor, called to see the unhappy girl, found her on a cot in a bare room. "Why do you live this way?" he asked her mother. "Because it suits us," she snapped. Another doctor threatened legal action unless Ocey got food. The Sisters sought to divert him on his next visit by announcing that Ocey had married her cousin, Fletcher Snead. She had, too. But the doctor was unimpressed by the marriage certificate and threatened to return with the police. That night, after five years at Soule College, the Wardlaws fled.

Ocey and Fletcher were dropped off in Louisville, where Ocey bloomed. The unlikely marriage was actually consummated, for the girl got pregnant. This was a signal for the return of the Sisters, who chased Fletcher to Canada and carried Ocey to another gloomy house in Brooklyn. The doctor who attended her pregnancy slipped her food, which she wolfed like an animal. Once the child was born, the doctor found himself locked out. He tried to climb in a window, but was thwarted by Virginia Wardlaw. He went to a lawyer who advised him to mind his business.

The unholy trio had no need for a baby. Telling Ocey the child was dead, they put it in a foundling home. Leaving Brooklyn, they moved to another big house in East Orange, New Jersey. Here a doctor found Ocey weeping for her child and decided she was drugged as well as famished. On November 29, 1909, a call to the local police reported Ocey a suicide. The cops found her lying in a bathtub with just enough water to cover her face. A small amount of water was found in her stomach, plus traces of morphine. The cause of death was starvation.

Police suspicions intensified when it was discovered that Ocey had long ago been insured for $32,000, with a premium paid just a few days before. The Three Sisters in Black were arrested and charged with murder. As if in penance, Virginia Wardlaw refused to eat and slowly died behind bars. Now there were only Two Sisters in Black. Brought to trial, Mrs. Martin and Mrs. Snead claimed innocence, stating that Ocey had become a morphine addict. The State called Ocey's mother murderously insane and said her two sisters had devoted their lives to keeping this hidden. The jury gave Mrs. Martin seven years for manslaughter, but set Mrs. Snead free. In prison, the behavior of Ocey's mother became so violent that she was moved to an asylum, where she died in 1913.

A girl who never had a chance, Ocey Snead was starved to death by her mother and aunts, one of them her mother-in-law. The Sisters piously called Ocey a chronic invalid.

26.
THE PLOT AGAINST CLARENCE DARROW

Clarence Darrow at his time of greatest crisis. Called a traitor to labor and accused of bribing potential jurors, the lawyer was nearly broke, almost friendless.

"The scabbiest town on earth," labor unions called Los Angeles in 1910. A citizen added, "The smiling, booming City of the Angels has become the bloodiest arena in the Western World."

One cause of this was Harrison Gray Otis, publisher of the Los Angeles *Times*. A bloodthirsty veteran of the Civil War, Otis was an enemy of all forms of progress. Fanatically opposed to labor unions and the closed shop, Otis organized a merchants-manufacturers association which proclaimed, "We employ no union men." The strikebreaking of Otis and his group became so vicious that, to fight back, labor resorted to bombs and dynamite. Otis, fearing for his life, strapped a small cannon to the running board of his car.

In the early hours of October 1, 1910, a huge explosion tore out a wall of the skyscraper housing the *Times*. Ink barrels caught fire and within minutes the structure was an inferno of flame so intense that rescue work was impossible. Twenty men, working overtime inside, were burned to death.

While fire hoses poured water on the blaze, Otis issued a statement saying the explosion was no accident. Organized labor, he charged, had placed dynamite in the building. Shortly two union-leader brothers, Jim and John McNamara, were arrested for the crime. The McNamaras,

Twenty men burned to death after a dynamite explosion ripped through the Los Angeles Times *building. The* Times *publisher, a rabid labor-baiter, immediately accused unions of the crime.*

The McNamara brothers, John and Jim, accused of the Los Angeles Times *dynamiting, were confident at the beginning of the trial. Darrow at first thought them innocent, slowly became convinced of their guilt. His turnabout ended his career as a labor lawyer.*

aged 27 and 28, were clean-cut and handsome. Not only labor, but most fair-minded Americans, decided that the two upstanding men were being framed. Unions and other groups collected funds for the defense of the brothers.

For this trial, there could be only one possible choice as lawyer. He was 53-year-old Clarence Darrow, who had left a lucrative corporation practice to become the nation's foremost defender of labor cases. "He turned cases into Causes," a writer said, explaining the homespun Darrow's ability to draw attention to his trials. In 1902 the nation had been swayed by Darrow's defense of striking anthracite coal miners. In 1907, he held newspaper readers enthralled through the trial of the labor leader Big Bill Haywood, charged with a bombing in Idaho. This long trial (and its longer preparation) had been a strain on Darrow. In Haywood and his militant Wobblies, Darrow also found himself aiding a group which believed dynamiting justified. This violated Darrow's

deep-seated principles. He had returned to Chicago determined never to accept another labor-murder case.

But pressures from the entire country pushed him toward the McNamaras. Promised a $50,000 fee, plus a $200,000 defense fund, Darrow reluctantly took the case. In Los Angeles, the big, shambling man found himself surrounded by confusion and trickery. The Otis forces, already using the staff of the Los Angeles D.A., had also called in the Burns Detective Agency. Burns and the D.A.'s men bribed Darrow's men, and Darrow could only bribe back. Both sides combed the country for evidence and bits of it brought Darrow to a tragic conclusion. He decided the McNamaras were guilty.

Now he faced a crucial decision. Should he continue on the case, if only in an attempt to save two lives? Or should he abandon it—which in hate-filled Los Angeles meant the gallows for the pair? Darrow's dilemma appeared solved by the

96

arrival of the crusading journalist, Lincoln Steffens, who nursed the visionary idea of pleading the McNamaras guilty, with a promise of life terms. As a result, Steffens thought, labor-management relations all over the country would improve. Darrow told him to speak to Otis, who grudgingly agreed. Just before the trial opened, the McNamaras rose in court to plead guilty.

The country reeled in shock, and Darrow was called a traitor to labor and justice. It then became apparent that Steffens' faith had been misplaced. Having got the McNamaras, Otis and his supporters wanted Darrow. The order went out, "Get Darrow." Shortly before the McNamara plea of guilty, a member of Darrow's staff made clumsy efforts to bribe two potential jurors. Money passed on a busy corner, in full view of city detectives. The law pounced and the briber swore Darrow had been behind the attempted bribe. The famous lawyer was arrested and held for trial.

Darrow waited six months for his trial to begin. He was still considered a betrayer of American labor and old friends shunned him. He had not received his $50,000 fee and funds dwindled. Knowing this, Otis and his group ordered the trial extended as long as possible. It ran three more months, filling eighty-nine bulky volumes of testimony. Darrow, in deep depression, felt he was in no shape to defend himself. He hired his legal opposite, flamboyant Earl Rogers, drinker

and *bon vivant.* Darrow's despair increased as he sensed Rogers also considered him guilty. Rousing himself, he gradually took over his own defense. Darrow spoke for a day and a half in a final eloquent plea. Yet it was Rogers who, in a few terse sentences, made the telling summation—

Will you tell me how any sane, sensible man who knows anything about the law business—and this defendant has been in it for 35 years—could make himself go to a detective and say to him: *Just buy all the jurors you want. I put my whole life, my reputation, I put everything I have into your hands. I trust you absolutely. I never knew you until two or three months ago and I don't know much about you now. But there you are. Go to it!*

The verdict was not guilty, but Los Angeles was not through with Darrow. He was arrested on a second bribery charge. After another long wait, he went through a trial which ended in a hung jury. Darrow was now out of funds, able to get back to Chicago only because an unknown benefactor mailed him $1,000. Home at last, Darrow announced that never again would he practice law. He became a lecturer on the Chautauqua circuit, but occasional court cases lured him back. Slowly, he turned lawyer again.

Yet Harrison Gray Otis and the labor-baiters won a victory. Now Clarence Darrow was a criminal lawyer. He never practiced as a labor-lawyer again.

On August 9, 1910, Mayor William J. Gaynor of New York, embarking on a trip to Europe, stood posing for photographers on the deck of the liner. As William Warnecke of the Evening World *clicked his camera a disgruntled city employee shot Gaynor. It made one of the most remarkable photographs in all history. First to recognize this fact was the* Evening World *city editor who exclaimed, "What a wonderful picture! Blood all over him—and exclusive too!"*

1910

27. AS THE CAMERA CLICKED

28. FINIS TO A NOVELIST

David Graham Phillips, handsome and hard-working, paid a fatal price for mere fiction.

David Graham Phillips was a broad-shouldered six-foot-three, with the rugged, strong-jawed handsomeness of the Gibson Man, beau ideal of the era. He dressed in extravagant fashion, wearing flowered waistcoats and large white chrysanthemums in his lapel. He also smoked cigarettes —in those days considered effete. But there was nothing soft about David Graham Phillips. He was an outstanding newspaperman who said, "I always write about the human beings involved in a story, no matter what."

He also said, "I'd rather be a reporter than President"—and meant it. Born in Indiana at a time when that state bristled with literary talent, Phillips decided at Princeton to become a newspaperman. Inevitably he was drawn to New York City, with its exciting newspaper hub on Park Row. He worked on the *Sun* and the *World*, the two top papers of the day. After ten years, journalism became less of a challenge. He decided that his next step was to write novels. "I will tell as accurately as I can, what I see," he vowed. In

1899, he published the *Great God Success,* about the *World* and its publisher, Joseph Pulitzer. It was popular and he soon quit newspaper reporting altogether.

As a novelist Phillips probably worked harder than any writer since Balzac. Like Balzac, he preferred working at night. In his large apartment on East 19th Street, around the corner from Gramercy Park, he began at 11 P.M., kept on until 6 A.M. or later. He labored seven nights a week, averaging 6,000 words a night. At that rate, he got far ahead of himself. "If I should die tonight," the handsome author liked to say, "I'd leave six years output behind."

Phillips' books were great popular successes, making him rich and famous. Yet for all his good fortune, he remained a cynic, which brought flavor to his work. His favorite target was the fair sex. "The American woman is hopeless," he wrote. "Her vanity is triple-plated, copper-riveted." In his best seller, *The Fashionable Adventures of Joshua Craig,* he directed his barbs at a flighty society girl. One reader of the novel was Fitzhugh Coyle Goldsborough, neurotic son of a wealthy Washington family. The single bright

Fitzhugh Coyle Goldsborough had decided that David Graham Phillips had maligned his sister in a best-selling novel. The girl had never even met Phillips.

spot in Goldsborough's brooding existence was a social butterfly sister, whom he adored. After finishing Phillips' novel, Goldsborough concluded that the novelist had patterned the heedless society girl on the real-life sister. His sister assured him she had never met Phillips, but it made no difference. Goldsborough became obsessed with the idea of killing the man who had so grievously wronged his sister.

In 1911, David Graham Phillips, aged 43, was better off than ever. He had just completed *Susan Lenox: Her Fall and Rise,* a book he considered his masterpiece. Yet he did not allow himself to relax. In the early hours of January 23rd, he finished a short story called *Enid.* He planned to mail it to the *Saturday Evening Post* during the day. Rising at noon, he put on one of the ornate, expensive suits for which he was famous. After breakfast he slipped into a fine raglan overcoat and started to walk toward Gramercy Park and the Princeton Club, on the north side. The Princeton Club had formerly been the residence of Stanford White.

The tall figure of Phillips was a familiar sight to nursemaids and children in the Park. The pale, jittery man apparently waiting for him on the sidewalk was not. This was, of course, Goldsborough. As Phillips approached, the young man suddenly confronted him, drawing a magazine-revolver from his pocket. Phillips stopped, nonplused. "Here *you* go," the young man yelled. He fired six times, moving his hand in a circle so that bullets struck Phillips between chest and knees. Three shots went through the manuscript of *Enid,* in the author's breast pocket, one of them piercing his right lung. As Phillips fell back to the Park fence, Goldsborough stepped to the curb, and lifted the pistol to his temple. "Here *I* go," he shouted and killed himself.

Phillips was helped to the Princeton Club, where he lay on a sofa only a foot from where Stanford White's coffin had reposed. He was taken to Bellevue Hospital, and it was announced he would live. He told police of receiving a telegram early that morning signed with his own name—it must have been sent by the young man who shot him. Next day the nation was stunned by the news that Phillips was dead. He himself had given the reason. "I can fight two wounds, but not six," he said weakly.

Susan Lenox, published in 1917, fulfilled the author's expectations. It was hailed as a masterpiece, but today it is almost forgotten.

1911

29. AN HEIRESS VANISHES

Dorothy Arnold vanished into thin air from Fifth Avenue and 27th Street, one of the busiest corners in the world. Hundreds of people surrounded her at high noon of a bleakly sunny November day. Yet not one saw anything happen to her—if anything did.

Twenty-five-year-old Dorothy was a New York society girl, but not a pretty, kick-up-her-heels type who would attract serious trouble. Rather than pretty, Dorothy was healthy looking. Her figure was stocky, her face wide and friendly with the over-all look of a studious Bryn Mawr graduate, which she was. But if Dorothy was not unusual in looks, she was in another way. At a time when shopgirls earned eight to ten dollars a week, rich girls were conspicuous for the clothes they wore. Dorothy was rich, and when last seen was attired in a fashionable tailor-made, hip-length coat over a skirt that was fringed at the bottom. On her feet were high-heeled, high-button shoes, whose suede tops extended halfway up her calves. In her hands she carried a large silver-fox muff and a small satin handbag.

But with all this finery, the hat was most arresting. It was a monstrous object of black velvet decorated with a cluster of red roses. Around the underside of the brim, ran a suggestion of scalloped lace. The formidable hat was a model then called the Baker, and it resembled nothing so much as an inverted dishpan.

So attired, Dorothy Arnold had descended the steps of her home at 108 East 79th Street at 11 o'clock on the morning of December 12, 1910. She had just told her mother of plans to spend the day shopping for a dress to wear at her younger sister's debut later that month. But if Dorothy was going shopping, she took her own time doing so. First she walked to Fifth Avenue, then turned south to walk twenty blocks to 59th Street, where she bought a box of candy at Park & Tilford's.

With the candy in her muff, she returned to Fifth Avenue for another long hike south. This took her thirty-two long blocks to Brentano's bookstore at 27th Street. Here she bought a book called *An Engaged Girl's Sketches,* by Emily Calvin Blake. On the sidewalk outside the bookstore, she next encountered a girl friend—as a New York society girl Dorothy had many. The two chatted spiritedly, promising to meet again at the upcoming debut of Dorothy's sister. Then they parted. After crossing Fifth Avenue, the other girl paused to wave back gaily to her friend.

No one ever saw Dorothy Arnold again. . . .

When she failed to return to 79th Street for dinner that night, her father, mother, sister, and brother telephoned friends. Dorothy had not been seen by any of them. People of the high social position of the Arnolds—Mr. Arnold's sister was the wife of Justice Peckman of the U.S. Supreme Court—never called in police or informed newspapers when in trouble. Instead, for six drawn-out weeks, the Arnolds used private detectives. Finally, the elder Arnold gave in and consulted the police. On January 22, 1911, he also summoned reporters to tell of the mysterious disappearance of his elder daughter. Grudgingly, her father admitted that Dorothy aspired to be a writer, an occupation he deplored. She had written several short stories, which had been rejected by magazines. As described by her father Dorothy's life appeared so stuffy that reporters pressed in to ask if she had been interested in men. At this Mr. Arnold erupted, "I do not approve of men who have nothing to do!"

Acting on this meaty tip, the press learned that Dorothy had been interested in George Griscom, Jr., a tubby 40-year-old who lived quietly with his parents on Philadelphia's Main Line. Now another bombshell burst, for it was learned that the summer before Dorothy had done something society girls never did in those proper days. After telling her family she was going to Boston to visit a Bryn Mawr classmate, she met Griscom instead. The two stayed at separate Boston hotels. At the end of a week, money ran out, and Dorothy pawned some jewels, in-

POLICE DEPARTMENT

CITY OF NEW YORK.

LOOK FOR --MISSING

Miss Dorothy H. C. Arnold
Of No. 108 East 79th Street
New York City

Circulars advertising Dorothy's disappearance were sent out after the Arnolds finally notified the police. Young enough to be still alive, Dorothy remains Card No. 1 in the Bureau of Missing Persons file.

Dorothy's mother and brother took a mysterious trip to Europe in an attempt to find her without calling in the police. Here the two debark after a futile journey.

George Griscom, Jr., a half-hearted suitor, preferred his mother to matrimony. Yet pictures show him cast down by Dorothy's disappearance.

scribing her right name on the hock-shop record. It was this pawnbroker who tipped off the press to her Boston visit.

Griscom, now in Naples with his parents, reported by cable that he knew nothing of Dorothy's disappearance. Meantime, the public was reading details of Dorothy's recent Thanksgiving sojourn with the classmate she had pretended to visit the summer before. Dorothy had arrived on Wednesday night prepared to spend the four-day holiday. On Thursday morning, a package came for her, though no mail is delivered on Thanksgiving. She tossed it carelessly aside, letting the classmate believe it was a rejected manuscript. On Friday, she astounded her friend by leaving. At 79th Street her family was equally astounded when she arrived home. "We thought you were staying till Monday," her mother said. Dorothy shrugged and went to her room, where she found letters with a foreign postmark, presumably from Griscom.

At the January 22nd press conference, Mr. Arnold stated that his wife, a semi-invalid, had gone to New Jersey to escape pressures. Now the semi-invalid turned up in Italy, where she and son John sought out Griscom. John and Griscom exchanged hot words, after which Griscom handed over a packet of letters. Griscom's return to the United States on February 11th produced nothing. He put "come-home" personal ads to Dorothy in newspapers, but there was no response. . . .

Dorothy Arnold never came back. Inevitably it was said that she had been pregnant, and died on an abortionist's table or jumped from an ocean liner or a Fall River boat. But though Dorothy was occasionally moody, she was not depressed before her disappearance. Nor was she a girl who would spoil her sister's debut by pulling a vanishing act. The most durable rumor about her says the Arnold family banished their pregnant daughter—the family disgrace!—to Switzerland. But as a Bryn Mawr graduate and a New York society girl, Dorothy knew many people who would travel in Switzerland and might recognize her. In more than fifty years she has never been seen there or anywhere.

Elegantly attired on the day of her disappearance, Dorothy carried a muff and pocketbook and on her head wore a modish Baker chapeau.

Swaggering and handsome, Charles Becker was called "the crookedest cop who ever stood behind a shield." He engaged in graft on a monumental scale.

United Press International Photo

1912

30. THE CASE OF THE CROOKED COP

I want Rosenthal croaked!"

Speaking was Police Lieut. Charles Becker, who seemed everything a fine law-enforcement officer should be. Handsome, ham-fisted, outgoing, known for a variety of sensational arrests, the 42-year-old Becker stood before an admiring New York public, his image polished by a paid press agent. Citizens slept better when they knew Charley Becker was enforcing the nighttime law, but the underworld knew a different man. This one was arrogant, brutal, and sadistic—a cop who, even as a beat-pounding patrolman twenty years before, had displayed a remarkable talent for ingratiating himself with his superiors. Now, in 1911, he easily charmed the newly appointed Police Commissioner, Rhinelander Waldo. First

Waldo made Becker a personal aide, then placed him in charge of a new Special Squad Number One.

While the bemused Commissioner preened himself on this move, Becker went to work transforming Special Squad Number One into a strong-arm squad. For behind his noble façade, Becker had always been a crooked cop. One Gay Nineties story has it that the novelist Stephen Crane wrote *Maggie: A Girl of the Streets* after seeing Becker's huge fists beat-up a young harlot who refused to give him part of her earnings.

As head of the new strong-arm squad, Becker still demanded a share of the profits of prostitution. But this was small stuff compared to the potential take from the wide-open gambling

104

which flourished from the gilded dens of Broadway to the stuss games of the lower East Side. Becker was determined to get a cut of every dollar gambled, and he got it. His men raided and demolished the premises of stubborn gamblers, or jailed them on fake evidence. His cops did the dirty work, but Becker commandeered the payoffs as personal tribute. To collect his graft, he built up a group of bagmen who might have stepped from a Chamber of Horrors. One was Jack Rose, called "Billiard Ball Jack" because he had no hair on his head. Another was "Big Jake" Zelig, mad-dog killer from the Ghetto. Others were Bridgie Weber, Sam Schepps, and Harry Vallon, who had a face like a meat ax. Becker gave full protection to this grimy group. "Nothing you do for me will get you in trouble with the law," he promised.

Becker was no shadowy, behind-the-scenes mastermind. In a tailored police uniform he rampaged the Great White Way, the sinful Tenderloin, tough Hell's Kitchen, the treacherous East Side. He was Uncrowned Law, hulking and awe-inspiring, calling gamblers, pimps, and prostitutes by their first names.

One gambler friend was Herman "Beansie" Rosenthal, who ran an ornate place named the Hesper on West 45th Street. The two were buddies at first, and Rosenthal gave Becker a share in the Hesper in return for his protection. But Becker couldn't stand pasty-faced Herman for long. Soon he was saying that the gambler talked too much and was a goddam coward. Conveniently forgetting he was part owner of the Hesper, he levied higher tribute on it. Beansie protested and the strong-arm squad raided his place, smashing fixtures to bits. A cop was put on guard outside the premises that night. Next day, Becker ordered a cop stationed twenty-four hours a day in the Rosenthal apartment. This gave Beansie's wife the jitters and drove Herman wild.

Serving as Republican District Attorney in a Democratic city was Charles S. Whitman, who dreamed of busting Becker and exposing the evils of the city's lid-off gambling. But he couldn't get evidence until the day word filtered upward that Herman Rosenthal was ready to talk. The two met and Beansie spewed out his hatred of Becker with names, dates, and a list of Becker's tough collection chain-of-command. The next step was to convene a Grand Jury to listen to Rosenthal's story.

Learning this, Becker gave a tight grin. He called in Billiard Ball Jack Rose and Big Jack Zelig, the East Side killer. Zelig provided four young gunsels, Gyp the Blood, Dago Frank, Lefty Louis, and Whitey Lewis. To them Becker said, "Kill him anywhere. Do it in front of a

105

policeman and it'll be all right. I'll take care of everything."

At midnight, July 21, 1912, Herman Rosenthal entered the Cafe Metropole, a gamblers' haunt on West 43rd Street. His appearance sparked one of the strangest scenes in crime history. By the Metropole code, Beansie was a lousy squealer. None present would speak to him as he moved from table to table, displaying a newspaper headlining his session with Whitman. "That's what the newspapers think of me," he babbled, pointing to his name in big black type. Those at the Metropole knew Beansie would never live to get

The Rosenthal murder, contrived with such vast arrogance, fell apart of its very carelessness. Becker had instructed the men at the local precinct to "lose" the license plate number of the getaway car if any citizen reported it. That, he thought, was all he needed to do. But he was thwarted by the speedy appearance of D.A. Whitman at the station house. Police tried to hide a man who knew the license number, but Whitman grabbed him. The trail of the getaway car led first to Billiard Ball Jack Rose, who after ten days in jail realized Becker would not lift a finger to help him. "I'm being thrown to the

United Press International Photo

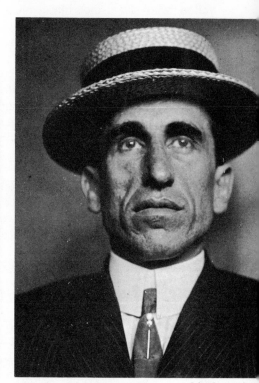

Culver Pictures, Inc.
Culver Pictures, Inc.

Becker's arrest opened up the underworld. One to crawl forth was Jack Rose (LEFT), known as Billiard Ball Jack because he was hairless. Gyp the Blood (real name, Harry Horowitz) was a trigger man on Becker's orders. Harry Vallon (RIGHT) ranked with Jack Rose as a top collector for Becker.

before a Grand Jury, but the thought never seemed to hit him. At 2 A.M. a voice from the street doorway called, "Herman, somebody wants to see you outside." Without a qualm, Rosenthal stepped to the sidewalk, standing momentarily blinded by the bright lights of the marquee. "Over here, Beansie," a voice called. Rosenthal moved toward it and four shots mowed him down. A gratuitous *coup de grâce* blew off the top of his head.

wolves," he decided. Rose sent for D.A. Whitman and began to talk. Gyp the Blood and his pals, hired so impersonally, had no loyalty to Becker to keep them silent. When caught, they talked too.

The four gunsels were tried and electrocuted. But even before their trial, evidence made Becker appear the real villain, a bigger-than-life-size crooked cop, symbol of police corruption. He too was placed on trial for murder, though he had not pulled a trigger or been at the murder

The Becker jury, kept isolated to prevent threats from the underworld, rode to and from hotel in a vintage omnibus. Significance of the swastika is unknown.

scene. He was found guilty and sentenced to death, but the court record showed such anti-Becker bias on the part of the judge that he got a second trial. Again he was guilty.

By now District Attorney Whitman had been elected Governor of New York. Becker's wife, who remained faithful to the end, bitterly composed a name-plate for the coffin. It read:

CHARLES BECKER
Murdered July 7, 1915
By Governor Whitman

Crowds waited outside court during Becker's two trials. He was found guilty at each. Becker was so strong physically that first jolts in electric chair failed to kill him. His execution is recalled as Sing Sing's clumsiest.

As American Citizens we ask you to join in the Protest against the injustice to an American Citizen.

Hang out an American Flag at half mast for Sympathy and Protest.

LEO. FRANK Protest League.

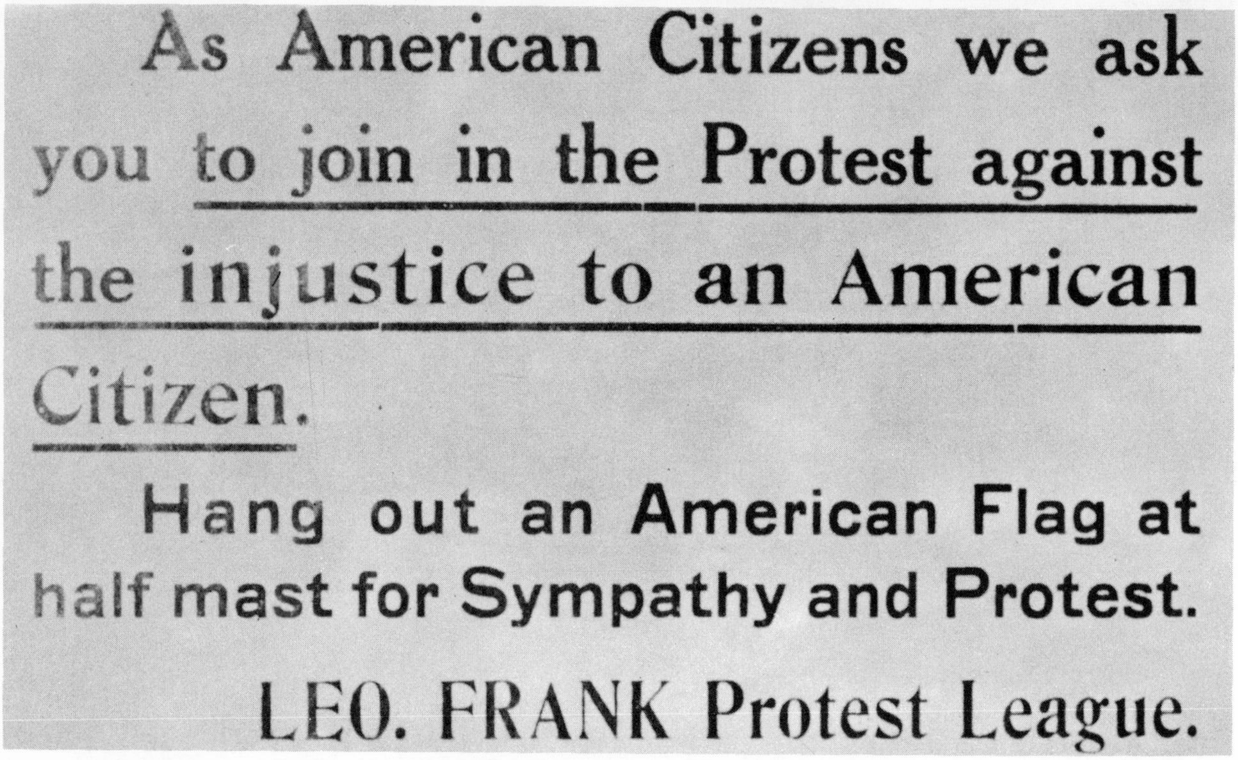

The anti-semitism involved in the Frank case aroused nationwide protest. Appeals like the one above influenced Georgia's governor but not Atlanta's mob.

1913

31. JUDGE LYNCH PRESIDING

The story of Leo M. Frank reads like a night-mare.

Frank was twenty-nine, sensitive—and a Jew. Born in Brooklyn, he graduated from Cornell, and married a girl of his own faith from Atlanta, Georgia. The girl's uncle, a Confederate veteran, owned a pencil factory in that city and brought Leo south to manage it. For five years Leo Frank did, living pleasantly with his wife and her parents, and active in local B'nai Brith.

Saturday, April 26, 1913, was Confederate Memorial Day, a holiday which shut the factory down. Leo, the Northerner, used the day to catch up on work in his second-floor office. At noon— by his story—a 14-year-old girl named Mary Phagan entered to ask for wages due. Mary was pretty and most fetchingly attired for the parade in lavender dress and blue hat. Frank did not know her by name and asked her payroll number. Mary supplied it and he gave her an envelope containing $1.20. Mary had been laid off during most of the past week because of a shortage in materials. Now she asked if new materials had arrived. "No," Frank answered. She left his of-fice, but apparently before leaving the building stopped to use the downstairs toilet.

Twenty-three hours later, Leo Frank was in custody, charged with the rape-slaying of Mary Phagan, whose body had been found in the fac-tory cellar by a night watchman. Mary had put up a fierce fight for her young life. Her face had been rubbed so hard in cinders that it was hard at first to tell if she were Negro or white. Appar-ently in the incredible belief that the world would

108

think Mary had written to her mother while being brutally assaulted, the killer left two illiterate notes beside her body. Addressed to "Mum," they described her murderer as "a long, tall, sleam, black negro . . . that long tall black negro did [it] buy his slef."

As the last person known to have seen Mary alive, Leo Frank instantly became Atlanta's Number-One suspect. He remained so, despite mounting proof of his innocence. The Southern city rose in mass delirium to picture him a vicious degenerate. Said one editorial: "Our little girl—*ours* by the eternal God!—has been pursued to a hideous death by this filthy perverted Jew from New York."

Leo Frank's worst offense was his being Jewish. Popular legend in the South said Jews were monsters, urged on by rabbis to violate girls of different faith. Besides, Leo Frank was a Northern Jew and Atlanta had become irate at Northern money taking over Southern industries. Other factors worked against him. Atlanta was suffering guilt feelings over girls of fourteen working a six-day week in factories. Also, Atlanta police were under fire after a recent crime wave had left them baffled. Police brass feared an official investigation if they failed to nab a killer. They knew exactly how the public felt, for a newspaper printed a front-page drawing of Mary's broken body with the heading SOLVE IT!

Brown Brothers

Leo Frank, quiet Atlantan, was convicted of killing a fourteen-year-old girl. His real offense was his Jewish blood, Northern upbringing.

Neglected in the Roman-holiday of hate was Jim Conley, Negro, short and squat (as opposed to the *long-sleam-tall* of the note), a sweeper in the factory who had reached second grade in school. Jim was on the premises the fatal Saturday, sleeping off a drunk in the safety of the stairwell. Police had found him washing a shirt which could have been bloodstained. Jim promptly cleared himself of all suspicion by swearing he could not write. At the end of a nightmarish week, Leo Frank heard this and said Conley *could* write. With this, Conley admitted writing the clumsy notes found next to the body, but claimed to have done so at Frank's direction. He said he often stood guard while Frank molested factory girls. Conley stated he had been in the factory office on Saturday when Frank hit Mary because she resisted him. The girl fell back, fatally striking her head. Conley ended by saying Frank had given him $200 to carry the body to the cellar and write the notes.

Frank's upstairs office showed no traces of blood or struggle. There was blood all over the cellar where Conley slept, perhaps waking on Saturday just as Mary entered or left the toilet. Yet for once a Negro's word was accepted over

Mary Phagan (ABOVE), *worked in Frank's factory. Collecting back pay on a day off, she was paid by Frank and never seen alive again.*

Mob spirit was built up by crowds (BELOW) *which gathered daily to discuss case in the squares of Georgia towns.*

Men who lynched Leo Frank proudly posed before the dead body. His sentence commuted to life imprisonment, Frank was kidnapped from the State pen, driven to this scene in Atlanta's suburbs.

a white man's. Conley was housed comfortably in police headquarters, where detectives helped him perfect his story.

At Leo Frank's thirty-day trial, lynch-law ran rampant. Mobs cheered the prosecutor, chanted at Frank's attorneys, "If the Jew doesn't hang, we'll hang *you*." By Georgia law a defendant could not testify under oath, but at the end of the trial Frank spoke informally in his own behalf. He did this with such dignity and conviction that the judge felt qualms of conscience. Even so, the mob-mood rose to such violence that Frank was not permitted in court to hear the verdict. He was found guilty and the joyous shouts of the crowds inside and out were so loud that the judge was unable to hear as he polled the jury. That night Atlantans cakewalked before the pencil factory.

Leo Frank's fate no longer hung on guilt or innocence, but on whether he deserved another trial because he had not been present to hear the verdict. At length the U.S. Supreme Court, Hughes and Holmes dissenting, called the trial legal. Leo Frank was sentenced to die on June 22, 1915.

Now the key man became Governor Straton. His own state still seethed with ugly mob spirit, but fellow governors pressured him in favor of Leo Frank, while letters and petitions in favor of clemency flooded his office. Straton rose to the occasion—he commuted the sentence to life imprisonment. "The reign of terror in Georgia is over," a Northern editorial said.

It wasn't. On an August night two months later, a group of prosperous looking men broke into the state penitentiary. They overawed, rather than overpowered, warden and guards, to carry Leo Frank on a ghastly 125-mile ride back toward Atlanta. At a spot near where Mary Phagan lived, a howling, gloating mob waited. There, one of the most unfortunate men ever born in the United States was lynched.

111

Erik S. Monberg

In the era before World War I, the United States provided a happy hunting ground for glib-tongued spielers selling everything from patent medicine to gold-bricks. (ABOVE), Harper's Weekly *artist Harold Matthews Brett shows a "professor" extolling his worthless wares.*

1913

32. NOTHING FOR SOMETHING

The Con Game is a uniquely American institution.

No other country has ever offered such fertile soil to the fast-talking swindler offering gold bricks, worthless stocks, or snake-oil remedies. No other country provided so many suckers, people eager to be bilked of life savings in return for the promise of quick riches. Between the turn of the century and World War I, golden-tongued spielers in cities succeeded in selling Brooklyn Bridge, the Chicago stockyards, and San Francisco City Hall. In rural districts, it was gold-mine stocks and watery patent medicines guaranteed to make the hair grow or bunions vanish. No, sir—for spielers on the one hand and rubes on the other, there has never been a country like the good old U.S.A. . . .

For proof, take Cassie Chadwick (see page 68). But no matter how great Cassie's triumph, the top native Con Man remains Joseph "Yellow Kid" Weil. A slight, lightning-witted citizen of Chicago, the Yellow Kid worked as an unabashed swindler for most of his eighty-plus years. He made, and lost, $8,000,000 from his inspired con games, most of which originated in his own fertile cranium. In time, the Yellow Kid became a famous figure in the Windy City, with reporters like Ben Hecht and Charles McArthur delighting in his nuggets of spoken wisdom. In the 1950's, the Yellow Kid wrote his autobiography with the help of W. T. Brannon. When the Federal Government held Chicago hearings on prevention of juvenile delinquency, this elder-statesman Con Man was one of the experts called to testify.

The Yellow Kid got his nickname from youthful addiction to a comic strip of that name—the pioneering Outcault cartoon which also gave a name to New York's War of Yellow Journalism. Son of hardworking parents, Joe Weil early made note of the small financial reward his father and mother got for their labor. At the same time, he observed that the rich seemed to grow richer by letting others work for them. Thus he evolved a lifetime philosophy. He would earn his money from the honest toil of others.

In 1913, Joe Weil was 36, a man at the top of his powers. He wore his honey-colored whiskers parted in the center and in every other way cut a dapper, dignified figure. The Yellow Kid could swindle on his own or stage-manage schemes which required the skilled casting and co-ordination of a Broadway show. Once, for instance, the Kid heard that the Merchants National Bank in Muncie, Indiana, was leaving its old building for a new one. Moving fast, he rented the old bank before the bank fittings could be removed. He then set about creating his own bank. First, he hired children to dash into the new bank, grab handfuls of deposit and withdrawal slips, carry them back to him. These he placed in the slots of his bank. He hired streetcar conductors in uniform to pose as guards and combed the Midwest for honest-looking crooks to act as tellers.

Joseph "Yellow Kid" Weil, the country's top con man, made millions, lived to pen his autobiography and testify as expert at Government hearings. No matter how great the stress, the Yellow Kid remained impeccable in manner and dress.

Meanwhile, he had been softening up an out-of-town millionaire, telling him a fine Muncie enterprise could be obtained cheap—for a mere $50,000. "Why, the president of the Muncie Bank vouches for it," Joe declared. The bank president was a dignified confederate of the Yellow Kid. Finally, the sucker was brought to Muncie to hear this from the bank president's own lips. The banker was busy and Joe and the sucker sat waiting for an hour. In that time, the bank teemed with well-rehearsed activity. (As customers, Joe had employed a motley group of touts, gamblers, and whores from local houses.) Bulging money bags were hauled across the floor, people deposited money or happily cashed checks. When the sucker finally reached the presence of the bank president, he was thoroughly softened.

The Yellow Kid was always at home in banks, his own and others. Later he posed as a millionaire Wall Streeter passing through Youngstown, Ohio. Making a courtesy call on the local bank president, he confided that he needed an hour to transact some private business. The bank president obligingly offered his private office. An hour gave Joe just enough time to pose as the bank president and fleece another human lamb.

Alone or with a supporting cast, Yellow Kid Weil was unbeatable. Once he read a magazine article about a man who took over an abandoned mine and made millions out of it. Joe carried the magazine to a counterfeiter friend who used his engraving equipment to recopy that page of the magazine, inserting Joe's picture in place of the man who made millions. Carefully rebound, the magazine looked good as new. The Yellow Kid then started to travel. In each new town, he planted his fake magazine in the local library. Posing as the subject of the story, he artlessly dropped name and date of the magazine. "You can find it in the library," he'd say, offhand. His victims wasted little time in looking it up. Joe never left any loose ends. After the swindle, he removed his copy of the magazine and put the right one back. Soon he was using his doctored copy in a new town.

The Yellow Kid had a fondness for champagne, Savile Row clothes, and brassy, willing girls. Yet he doted on a demure little wife who never ceased begging him to go straight. When Joe did, he always went broke and returned quickly to swindling on a lofty scale. He served several terms in Federal prisons (only the best for *him!*), seeming to enjoy incarceration as much as he did all of life. "I never cheated an honest man, only rascals," he told Saul Bellow, late in life. "They may have been respectable, but they were never any good. They wanted something for nothing. I gave them nothing for something."

Patent medicines were available for man or beast. Ads like this make amusing reading today, but at the time were taken seriously.

San Francisco demonstrated its readiness to fight World War I with this parade on Market Street on a Saturday afternoon in 1916. The bands played, crowds cheered until an explosion seemed to start the war on the spot.

1916

33. THE BOMB AT THE PATRIOTIC PARADE

The parade became a deadly shambles at corner of Market and Steuart Streets with ten killed and fifty wounded. Police found bits of black bag containing explosive.

It seemed that all San Francisco had turned out for the parade that Saturday afternoon....

The United States was reaching the peak of patriotism that led to involvement in World War I. President Wilson might still be clinging to the doctrine of Too-Proud-To-Fight and a popular song was "I Didn't Raise My Boy To Be A Soldier," but slowly the patriotic fever was rising. Only labor could be accused of dragging heels. Some American labor leaders had spoken out against war in principle, others called it

Labor leader Tom Mooney, accused of planting the bomb, was sentenced to death. Trial evidence proved to be perjury, but Mooney waited twenty-two years behind bars for pardon.

wasteful. To a flag-waving country this made labor partisans appear like traitors—or cowardly slackers prepared to evade any draft.

But few San Franciscans bothered to think of labor on the afternoon of July 22, 1916. A great Preparedness Day parade was proving that this West-Coast city was never too proud to fight. Army and militia units swung down Market Street to the rousing music of military bands. Suddenly at the intersection of Steuart Street

came a thunderous, flaming roar. When the pungent smoke cleared away, fifty spectators lay mangled on the street. Ten were dead or dying.

It took no mastermind to figure that a bomb had exploded. Police quickly found evidence that a suitcase containing explosives had been placed against the wall of a saloon on the corner. But who would do such a thing? For five days detectives labored and grew increasingly baffled. Then a group of conservative businessmen arrived at police headquarters with their version of what had happened....

The focus of California's labor strife had swung from Los Angeles to San Francisco, but the pattern resembled that of Los Angeles in McNamara-trial days. Local business leaders, in terror of unions, tried to kill them off by any means. With labor accused of being unpatriotic, new flame had been added to the anti-labor fire. In the minds of powerful San Franciscans it all added up: the bomb must have been placed by a labor agitator.

Police bought the idea, whether reluctantly or not history fails to record. In the light of later evidence, it appears that all parties concerned next sat down to choose the labor leader they liked least. The honor went to Tom Mooney, truculent iron-molder who had led strikes and advocated violence in settling labor disputes. Mooney was 32, married to an attractive girl named Rena. He also had a 22-year-old protégé, Warren Billings, who had once been convicted in a bomb plot. It seemed a neat solution to the whole problem to accuse Mooney and Billings of setting the bomb.

Mooney had an alibi. Like any loyal American, he had been watching the parade—from the roof of the Eilers building, 6,008 feet from the scene of the explosion. Besides, he had a photograph of himself and Rena watching the parade. In the background was a clock. If the clock told the right time, as presumably it did, Tom Mooney could not have been the one who left the bomb.

Police shoved this formidable alibi aside in favor of one Frank C. Oxman, self-styled "honest cattleman" from Oregon. Oxman swore that he had been standing at the corner of Market and Steuart Streets just before the parade and watched Mooney and Billings place a satchel against the saloon wall. Before leaving, the two men stood up, allowing him a perfect view. Mooney uttered the melodramatic words, "We must run away, the cops will be after us." Then they fled.

Oxman's straightforward testimony was enough to get death sentences for Mooney and Billings. Then came sensation! The honest cattleman, it transpired, was a liar—a perjurer on a gigantic scale. At the time of the explosion he had been ninety miles from San Francisco. Mooney's sentence had already aroused wide protest in labor circles, but now the outrage rose to national proportions. President Wilson appointed an investigating committee which concluded, "The utilities sought to get Mooney . . . with Oxman discredited, the verdict against Mooney was discredited."

With this, the sentences were commuted to life imprisonment and it was expected that pardons would follow. But Tom Mooney remained in prison for the next twenty-two years, and Billings longer. Why? Largely because California's archaic laws prevented consideration of perjury evidence after a verdict had been rendered. At the same time, the state's lawyers or public officials seemed afraid to make efforts to cut through the red tape enshrouding the old laws—perhaps from fear of being branded pro-labor. Public apathy in California has been attributed to unwillingness to believe that the law processes in a great state could go so far awry. At one point, Mayor James J. Walker of New York took a much-publicized trip to offer an insouciant plea for Mooney's freedom. Mooney himself confused matters by refusing parole, insisting on a full pardon.

Not until 1939 did he get it. Billings, as a previously convicted man, was in jail several years more. On the day Mooney was freed, he rode triumphantly up and down San Francisco streets while thousands cheered, much as they had at the Preparedness Day parade in 1916. Nor had truculent Tom changed. The day following his return, he joined a picket line in front of a local department store.

Warren K. Billings, convicted with Mooney, grew up on Dean Street, Brooklyn. Freed after Mooney, he returned to muse on the old family porch.

117

1919

34. LITTLE
CHARLEY
FOOLS
THE WORLD

Picture of a jaunty man, Charles Ponzi had evolved a gimmick which fooled millions. An immigrant, he turned specious coupons into gold for himself and his family.

Charles Ponzi was a little man—five-foot-two in height, one-ten in weight.

But he was a giant of gall and conceit, which qualities propelled him in eight stupendous months from lowly clerk to millionaire and bank president. He also attained a kind of immortality. People today have forgotten exactly what Ponzi did, but his name lives on as a symbol of financial trickery.

Ponzi came to this country from Italy, a boy immigrant convinced that America was the Land of Opportunity. It wasn't, at first. The best job he could get was that of waiter, and here the garrulous little chap ruined his chances by talking to the people he served. He went to Montreal, where money seemed to stretch further. On odd jobs he was able to indulge a fondness for tight-waisted suits, malacca canes, and long cigarette holders. He was glib—to say the least!—and began talking friends into letting him send money

118

The successful Ponzi drove his wife to this $100,000 mansion outside Boston. "It's ours," he said and promptly bought it.

to relatives in Italy at bargain rates. He lived high on the money given him, sent none back home. Soon he was in jail.

Ponzi was thirty-six when he arrived in Boston, as buoyant, dapper, and optimistic as if he had never been inside a prison. He met and married a pretty girl named Rose and persuaded her father to let his son-in-law manage his wholesale grocery business. Ponzi ruined this in record time. He then used his knowledge of Italian to get a $16-a-week job as a translating clerk for J. P. Poole, an import-export firm. Ponzi didn't like sitting at a desk all day, and his boss didn't like *him*. But he stuck it out until June 1919, when a postal-reply coupon crossed his desk. These were bought overseas for one cent, redeemed here for five cents. Ponzi had never heard of them—who had?—but decided that his path to fortune had opened. He quit the job to spend intoxicating hours outlining to Rose plans to subsidize agents abroad who would buy the postal-replies in quantity, then send them to Ponzi to redeem at a five hundred per cent profit. But when he tried this, the little dreamer discovered postal regulations made it impossible.

Still, he had a fistful of official-looking coupons, which he displayed to friends just as if the scheme could work. Cleverly, he intimated that the vast Rockefeller fortune was based on precisely the same gimmick. "Lend me fifty dollars," he urged. "I'll pay you back in ninety days, with fifty per cent interest." Few could resist and over three months he took in $1,250, paying back $750 on the first due date. "Re-invest," he told those he paid back. Then he said, "Tell your friends."

The little man was borrowing from Peter to pay Paul, but it worked. He transformed himself into the Financial Exchange Company and opened an office in the Boston financial district. At first, lines of people gathered outside to press money on him. Then, crowds. Ponzi took in over $3,000 a day and sat with his feet on a straw suitcase crammed with greenbacks. Soon he had so much money that he changed the pay-back period from ninety to forty-five days. Everything was done with a wide, beaming Ponzi smile. "You are the greatest Italian in history," people shouted at him. Ponzi had an outsize ego, but he couldn't accept this. "Columbus was the greatest," he called back. "Didn't he discover America?"

Charley had a wonderful time—for a while. He spent $12,000 on a chauffeur-driven Locomobile limousine. In it, he drove a dazzled Rose to Lexington where they stopped to admire a $100,000 mansion. "It's ours," he told her. Rose fainted. Ponzi had always been fascinated by banks, though banks had no use for him. Now he bought enough of the Hanover Trust Company to get himself elected president. He next bought the J. P. Poole Company and fired his old boss.

State officials, from Gov. Calvin Coolidge down, seemed awed by the cocky little manipulator. *Everybody's happy, so we'll let things alone,*

The whole family basked in Charley's happy glow. Italian-born Ponzi had few relatives here, but wife Rose had plenty.

seemed to be the official attitude. Only the Boston *Post* dared query the source of Ponzi's mysterious funds. It was a mild query, but Ponzi seemed upset by it. He wanted all the world to love him and hired public relations man William McMasters to achieve this. It was a mistake. McMasters talked to Ponzi and found he could barely add two and two. As to foreign exchange and high finance—why, he didn't comprehend the simplest financial procedures. McMasters went to state authorities and urged them to examine Ponzi's books. They looked at the few books Ponzi kept and found a madhouse hodgepodge. The whole scheme exploded.

Now crowds gathered to revile Ponzi. The desperate little fellow went to the Hanover Trust Company and packed $2,000,000 from the vault into the faithful straw suitcase. His chauffeur drove him in the Locomobile to Saratoga Springs, where he fully expected to win more millions at the gambling tables. In three days he was broke. Back in Boston, officials estimated that he had taken in about $20,000,000 and paid back $15,000,000 in the course of his operations. The balance of $5,000,000 were payments he would never be able to meet.

Ponzi sat disconsolately in his mansion waiting for Federal, state, and city authorities to close in. The Government got him first because Rose, who helped at the office, had used the mails to remind people to pick up money. Ponzi got five

United Press International Photo

Whatever goes up has to come down. Expression on face of secretary Lucy Meli shows how fast Ponzi was falling.

years in the Federal pen, served three. The State gave him seven more for grand larceny. By then Rose was through and when deported to Italy Ponzi traveled alone. Benito Mussolini made an attempt to use his rare talents but he too found out that, aside from colossal self-confidence, Charles Ponzi had nothing. The little man died in poverty in Rio de Janeiro in 1949.

Still, from December 20, 1919, to August 13, 1920—Friday the 13th!—Charles Ponzi was one of the most amazing men in the world. They can't take that away from him. . . .

Once crowds gathered to press money on Ponzi. Now they demanded it back. The desperate little man made a spectacular attempt to re-coup at gaming tables, was a mere $5,000,000 short.

United Press International Photo

Stunned, Bartolomeo Vanzetti and Nicola Sacco (RIGHT) sat manacled after being arrested on murder charges.

1920

35. SACCO-VANZETTI

Scene of the hold-up, pictured in a Boston newspaper, showed auto at spot where the killers' car stopped. "A" indicates point where the guard was killed and the cashier wounded. One gunman was concealed at "B." "C" shows where the wounded cashier fell in his dash toward him.

The Sacco-Vanzetti case eventually aroused violent controversy in the United States. Because of it, crowds also rioted before American embassies in Rome, Paris, Geneva, and other world capitals. Yet at the beginning few noticed. Far from having world wide implications, the hold-up that constituted the crime was most remarkable for movie-melodrama overtones.

It all began on April 15, 1920, with two men lounging against a fence opposite the Slater & Morrill Shoe Factory in South Braintree, just

Webster Thayer, presiding judge at the trial, was to many the villain of case. He hated foreigners and made no secret of it.

outside Boston, Mass. One man wore a cap, the other a felt hat. As Frederick Parmenter, factory paymaster, and a guard named Berardelli passed with the cash to meet the weekly payroll, the man in the cap suddenly stopped lounging. He hurled himself on Berardelli and the two grappled until the attacker drew a gun and fired three shots into the guard. Then he turned to fire twice at Parmenter, fatally wounding him. As he did, his partner in the felt hat ran about the street retrieving the boxes containing the $15,776.51 payroll. To protect him, the man in the cap pegged two shots at an eyewitness who ran forward to intervene.

At this moment of suspense a Buick touring car, its rain curtains flapping wildly, tore into view. Three men rode in it, one on the running board. As the car screeched to a stop, this man leaped off and ran to the prostrate body of Berardelli, firing a shot into it. Then he sprayed bullets

at the factory windows. By now the two original gunman were in the Buick. The fifth man jumped back on the running board and fired one last shot as the car roared away.

Speeding through South Braintree, the killers all but shot up the town. The wild man on the running board fired at passers-by and shouted in unaccented English, "Why don't you get out of the way, you son of a bitch." To a railroad-crossing watchman lowering his gate, he yelled, "What the hell are you trying to stop us for?" Meanwhile, two men in the back seat tossed tacks out the rear window to discourage pursuit.

The payroll holdup at Slater & Morrill, leaving two men dead, became a matter of identification. Who were the five men? Who, in particular, were the vicious pair who began it? This problem tumbled directly into the lap of Police Chief Michael E. Stewart of South Braintree, a man who wholeheartedly subscribed to the beliefs of A. Mitchell Palmer, then Attorney General of the United States, that foreign-born Reds—or Anarchists—were plotting to overthrow the American government. South Braintree had a large Italian population, most of them uninterested in taking out American citizenship. With extreme diligence Chief Stewart had cooperated with the U.S. Immigration Service in ferreting out South Braintree Italians who—he thought—should be deported as subversive.

One man he successfully hounded was named Ferucio Coacci, a former Slater & Morrill employee now working in a local foundry. Thanks to the efforts of Chief Stewart, Coacci was scheduled for deportation in a few days. Meantime he had failed to show up for work on April 15th, sending word that he was sick. Said Chief Stewart later, "Something hit me, the dates involved, the hold-up . . . the phony illness." His instinct told him that Coacci had been involved in the Slater & Morrill hold-up.

By the time Chief Stewart was ready to act on this flash of intuition, Coacci was on the high seas. Nonetheless, the police chief visited Coacci's former living quarters and found Mike Boda, whom he later recalled as a "smooth, suave individual." Chief Stewart switched his suspicions from Coacci to Boda. Learning this Boda left town, abandoning his Overland car. Stewart ordered the car watched. On May 5th, Boda returned for the car. With him were two foreign-looking strangers. Alerted by telephone, Chief Stewart ordered the arrest of the three. Again

United Press International Photo

Nicola Sacco was devoted to his wife and son Dante. Yet police tied him to the murder pistol, and 1962 book, Tragedy in Dedham, *makes the same charge.*

Boda vanished but the other two, walking slowly toward a trolley line, were easily arrested. They were Bartolomeo Vanzetti, itinerant fish peddler around the suburbs of Boston, and Nicola Sacco, shoemaker in a local factory.

Both men had been born in Italy. They barely spoke English, had never bothered to apply for American citizenship. Vanzetti, thirty-three, had been in this country fifteen years. While he peddled fish, he also handed out anarchist leaflets advocating a kind of idealistic revolution which has been called "noble nonsense." Sacco, mild and unobtrusive, joined the stronger Vanzetti in the belief that all governments should be overthrown—but by force of ideas rather than bombings. The two men were carrying revolvers when arrested, Sacco's being the type of .32 that fired bullets into Berardelli. With A. Mitchell Palmer in Washington, these were bad days for anarchists—even the philosophical type—and the two had decided that guns were necessary when they borrowed Boda's car to dispose of a batch of the leaflets Vanzetti passed out with his fish. In the station house, the two also seemed to lie. At the same time, they spoke broken English and later

Crowds mobbed Boston Common on August 23, 1927, the day of Sacco and Vanzetti's execution. City was an armed camp, while overseas crowds stoned American embassies.

said they had no idea Chief Stewart was questioning them about the South Braintree hold-up. Yet Stewart has said, "In my own mind, I believe that the men who committed that atrocious crime knew no God and had no regard for human life. Anarchists fit the bill and Sacco and Vanzetti were anarchists."

Sacco and Vanzetti were mild men, not likely to indulge in the mayhem and murder of the South Braintree job. None of the holdup money was found on them. Vanzetti was tall with a bravura mustache. Sacco was short. Witnesses said the two men lounging against the fence were equal in height. No one mentioned a heavy mustache. Still, the two were charged with participating in the crime.

"A murder trial is the supreme drama of the American courtroom," says writer Fred J. Cook. Though the payroll murders had failed to attract much attention, District Attorney Katzmann devoted his full energies to convicting Sacco and Vanzetti. Much went on behind the scenes before the trial. In April 1920, most of the eye-witnesses had said, "I didn't get much of a look," when asked to describe the killers. A year later, in May 1921, they mounted the witness stand to identify the two men without hesitation. A cap found at the scene was laboriously traced to Sacco. Yet when put on his head, it didn't fit. Fingerprints taken from the murder car with much newspaper fanfare vanished and are still the object of search. Outside the court, the State ballistics expert said, "They've got the wrong men." On the stand, he was asked only if Sacco's gun and the murder gun were .32's.

A curious aspect of the State's case was the attempt to prove Sacco and Vanzetti *four* of the five robbers. Sacco was first identified as the man in the cap who did most of the shooting. Then he became the man on the running board who shouted profanity in unaccented English as the

United Press International Photo

123

The protest reached an eloquent moment as crowds stood with bowed heads during the Sacco-Vanzetti funeral procession.

car roared through town. Vanzetti was first named as the man in the felt hat who picked up the money, then as driver of the car which arrived on the scene.

In all this, Prosecutor Katzmann got a heroic assist from Judge Webster Thayer, who presided at the trial. The Judge's everyday conversation was laced with references to "wops," "dagoes," "Italian sons of bitches," and slurs on other minority groups. His charge to the jury was a flag-waving, hate-spewing oration against foreigners, which practically ordered the twelve men to find the defendants guilty. Wrote Frank J. Sibley of the Boston *Globe,* "His whole manner, his whole attitude, seemed to be that the jurors were there to convict these two men." The jury did—though it took six hours of deliberation to do so.

Following the trial, Judge Thayer demanded of admiring friends, "Did you see what I did to those anarchist bastards?" As much as anything, his loose talk served to bring the case to world-wide attention. One who heard Judge Thayer's words was Robert Benchley, drama critic for the humor magazine, *Life.* He became so indignant that he filed an affidavit of protest. Largely through him such literary figures as Heywood Broun, Dorothy Parker, Edna St. Vincent Millay, and John Dos Passos joined the cause to free the condemned pair, spreading the word that injustice might have been done.

Legal briefs and appeals in the case took up months, then years. At one point, evidence came to light which tied the notorious Morelli gang of robbers to the South Braintree hold-up. Judge Thayer refused to re-open the case to examine it. After more than five embattled years, the Judge's final official act was to sentence the two men to

the electric chair in July 1927. With this came such loud protest that Governor Alvan Fuller postponed execution a month and appointed a commission headed by President A. Lawrence Lowell of Harvard to re-examine evidence. Much new testimony was heard by the commission. Yet all that seemed important to its members was the fact that Massachusetts justice was being questioned. In 1921, twelve good Massachusetts men and true had brought in a verdict of guilty. The committee, feeling this sufficient, upheld the execution date. "Not many prisoners have the President of Harvard throwing the switch for them," wrote Heywood Broun.

Sacco and Vanzetti's final days mounted to tense drama. The entire world watched as fruitless appeals were made to vacationing justices of the U.S. Supreme Court. On Monday, August 23, 1927—a date many consider Massachusetts' day of infamy—Boston resembled an occupied city. For the first time in history, the Common was closed to orators. Edna St. Vincent Millay and others marched as pickets, while Boston police ranged the city arresting other protesters. Riot squads with automatic rifles, hand grenades, and tear gas broke up street corner meetings.

Charlestown Prison, with its menacing electric chair, was a beleaguered fortress as night fell. Searchlights, machine guns, and fire hoses protected prison walls. At midnight, Sacco and Vanzetti stoically moved toward the death chamber, where Vanzetti paused to say, "I want to tell you that I am innocent and that I never committed any crime, but sometimes sin. . . . I wish to forgive some people for what they are doing to me."

Within minutes the executioner had twice pulled his switch.

36. DEATH OF A LADIES' MAN

Young Joseph B. Elwell found himself facing a moment of truth shortly after playing cards for the first time. He was nearly twenty, a native of Cranford, N.J., who had displayed a phenomenal memory in school but never made much of it. Now he had left school to become a hardware salesman in Brooklyn. Oddly, the personable young man had never before played cards. Tonight, playing with other salesmen, he found that just holding the pasteboards brought him a full measure of happiness, while the cards themselves seemed to respond to his every whim.

Though he couldn't put it into words at the time, Joe Elwell was a genius at cards, a card-playing wizard, so good that he soon decided to make card-games his livelihood. Now he faced his moment of truth. He could decide to play poker and such robust games with men, in the hope of someday owning his own gambling casino. Or he could choose gentler games like whist, which brought contact with women. The young man unhesitatingly chose the second, for no less than a wizard at cards, Joe Elwell was a ladies' man.

At first life was a struggle, but things became easier after 1904 when he married Helen Darby, whose social position and inherited income of $35,000 a year opened doors wide to him. Helen wrote *Elwell on Bridge* and *Elwell's Advanced Bridge,* books on which his name appeared. She

Joseph B. Elwell (on horseback) got mileage out of his fame as bridge expert. He owned a racing stable, a yacht, cars, an art collection. Still, his big interests were women and cards.

also polished his shaky grammar and table manners. But one woman was never enough for Joe. As a bridge authority, he lectured and gave private lessons. This surrounded him with women and, through them, their daughters. After ten trying years, Helen left. It made no difference to Joe. As auction bridge was supplanted by contract bridge his two books became national best sellers. All across the country, bridge-table arguments were settled by the words, "Elwell says . . ." Declares one expert, "He made bridge *the* indoor sport."

In 1920, Joseph Elwell was a debonair forty-four, a spruce-looking man with regular features, a long handsome face, fine wavy hair, glistening teeth, and an open, ingratiating manner. His books and lectures gave him a rich man's income and he made the most of it, with a yacht, five

Elwell's books, ghosted by his wife, brought him fame, fortune, and women to supplant her.

Dapper Joe never dropped his man-about-town front—even while on a beach.

automobiles, a 20-race-horse stable in Kentucky, and a valuable collection of Chinese *objets d'art*. He lived alone in a brownstone house at 244 West 70th Street, where a top-floor room served as a seduction chamber. Drawers were packed with lingerie for girls to wear home after a night of bliss. Elwell, who seduced on a grand scale, often found himself facing angry fathers, husbands, and brothers. He was called many nasty names, but matters never seemed to go beyond that.

For all his fancy tastes, Joe felt most at home amid the bright lights of Broadway. Here he was a showy dresser and willing spender, a familiar sight at first nights and ringside tables in cabarets. On the night of June 10, 1920, he moved, as always, in top Broadway circles. In black tie, he dined at the Ritz with Mr. and Mrs. Walter Lewisohn and Miss Viola Kraus, who was Mrs. Lewisohn's young sister. After dinner, the cheery foursome went to the New Amsterdam Roof for a performance of *Ziegfeld's Midnight Frolics*. Here they met a South American friend, who joined the party. After the show, the five tried to crowd into one taxi, but it couldn't be done. The others were going east. Elwell, the only west-sider, bowed out and took another cab home.

At two-thirty, Miss Kraus phoned to apologize for something she had said—or did the young girl merely want an excuse to speak to the ladies' man? He laughed off her apologies and the two

126

An old man sat bleeding to death in this chair. It was Joe Elwell, minus fine toupee and store teeth that made him a ladies' man.

head seemed to be too heavy a model for a woman to fire so accurately. A card index of women was found among the dead man's effects, and detectives laboriously investigated them all, ending several marriages in the process. Because he was without teeth or hair (a collection of forty toupees was found in a hidden closet), it was surmised that Elwell was talking to an intimate friend when killed. But Elwell was monumentally vain. It is unlikely he considered anyone intimate enough to see him bald and toothless.

Detective Inspector Cary, who handled the case, came to the prosaic conclusion that a robber had entered the house and was discovered by Elwell when he came down for the mail. But Elwell was seated when killed. An intruder bumping into the owner of a house as he sat reading a letter would hardly shoot to kill. It is more likely that he would run out the front door.

talked for a few moments. She sensed somebody was with him, decided it was a man. Phone company records showed that several hours later Elwell—who apparently hated going to bed—placed two unanswered calls to his horse trainer. At 6 A.M. the milkman deposited his bottles outside, and at seven-twenty the postman delivered mail, noting the front door was ajar. At eight, Mrs. Marie Larsen, housekeeper, arrived on schedule. The door was shut. She opened it, heard labored breathing. Slumped in a chair in a small reception room off the front hall was an old man, blood dripping to his lap from a bullet hole in mid-forehead. Through her horror, Mrs. Larsen recognized her employer, minus the fine hair and glistening teeth which she—no less than the rest of the world—thought his own. Elwell was rushed to a hospital where he died without regaining consciousness.

His murder was the perfect crime. In his lap was a letter left by the postman, so Elwell must have been shot between 7:20–8 A.M. Streets were light by then, but no one saw the killer. At first it was thought a woman must have done it, but the .45 revolver which shot the bullet through his

Elwell's murder made headlines, and reporters crowded the stoop of the New York brownstone in which he had lived.

127

The famous statue of George Washington stood unscathed after the bomb explosion in Wall Street at high noon of a business day. Thirty were killed, two hundred injured.

37. THE WALL STREET EXPLOSION

The bells of Trinity Church tolled noon as a decrepit rust-brown wagon pulled by a tired bay horse stopped in front of the U.S. Assay Building, opposite J. P. Morgan and Company, in the heart of Wall Street.

Even in 1920 a horse and wagon made a rare sight in New York's financial district and many of those on the street for lunch this September 16th looked curiously at the anachronism. But those in a position to see it best never lived to tell whether the driver of the old nag tossed reins over the animal's neck and disappeared, or whether he sat patiently on the seat of the wagon awaiting his doom. For at one minute after noon, with the Trinity bells still tolling, the innocent-looking wagon erupted into an explosion as terrible as any on a field of battle. . . .

A horrendous roar—it was heard ten miles away—ripped through the narrow, zigzag canyons of Wall Street. For a split second a cloud of saffron gas hung over the spot where horse and buggy had been, then out from under it roared a disc of flame. With it came a murderous barrage of death-dealing metal, for the mad hand which wrought this bomb had put it in the wagon and then smothered it with 500 pounds of window weights, carefully sliced into tiny bits. The Wall Street bomb was no accident. Its purpose was to kill and maim. . . .

The cloud of smoke lifted to reveal a 100-foot area choked with the dead, dying, and hideously mangled bodies. Those closest to the wagon had been completely blown to bits, others lay with skulls smashed and limbs ripped off, their screams filling the void left by the departing roar of the bomb. Horse and wagon had been blasted to smithereens—one hoof of the horse lay in the center of a pool of blood. Awnings twelve stories above had caught fire and wads of flame drifted lazily to the street. Every window in the bomb area had been blown out, while others half a mile away were shattered. Over the holocaust fell a moment of inexplicable silence during which, in the words of reporter Edmund Gilligan, "The gentle sound of tinkling glass falling and slipping from sill to ledge and thence to the pavement came like music." The eerie quiet ended as abruptly as it began, shattered by a girl's piercing cry of agony.

Those near the blast who were still able to stand had broken eardrums, shocked senses, or both. At first, when the gas cloud lifted, they moved back from the sight of blood and death before them. The girl's frantic scream seemed to stop this retreat. Those in front moved forward, partly in fascination, partly out of desire to help.

Far in the distance the sound of the blast reverberated among the tall buildings. About 100,000 people were in the Wall Street district at the time and from windows came shouts of "What happened—what was it?" In offices plaster had fallen and broken glass covered floors. Many workers had been cut by flying glass. The J. P. Morgan office was devastated, with chief clerk Thomas Joyce lying dead on the floor. Across the street, the statue of George Washington before the Subtreasury was miraculously unscathed. Thousands from the offices began pouring into the streets, trying to locate the cause of the blast. As they pushed toward Wall Street these crowds shoved those in the front rank forward so that they trampled the injured.

Yet the mob remained tractable, a fact later attributed to the sobering stench of gas in the area. Rescue units appeared with unusual rapidity and the thousands of the crowd formed lanes to permit entrance of police, doctors, ambulances, and fire trucks. Doctors and nurses ministered to two hundred injured, while thirty bodies were lifted into the mortuary wagon. Police pushed back the crowd to allow detectives to crawl on hands and knees in search of bits of bomb, wagon, horse, or driver. At night the scene was silent, with Federal troops in charge.

The bomb sent five hundred pounds of chipped sash weight shrapnel-like through the air. Autos nearby were reduced to metal skeletons, windows a half-mile away shattered.

Brown Brothers

129

New York police took the Wall Street bomb as a special challenge and worked with great diligence to solve the mystery. Horse and wagon were re-created and pictures of both shown in 5,000 stables around the eastern part of the country. Grass from the horse's stomach was analyzed, but told nothing except that it was country grass. The hunt was further snarled by the many cranks and fanatics eager to confess to bombing the money temples of Wall Street. The Red-baiters in evidence with Sacco and Vanzetti were also heard from, deriving support from a blacksmith who claimed to recall the wagon and said it was driven by a sinister Sicilian. Others claimed the bomb had been planted by the Irish Sinn Fein. A reward of $100,000 was posted. It should have helped, but did not.

For many years after, any New York detective who performed brilliantly on another crime was handed the file on the Wall Street bombing in the hope that a flash of inspiration might result. None ever did, and gradually the only hope became a deathbed confession.

So far, it hasn't come.

Brown Brothers

This overturned car at the center of the explosion was ripped inside and out. The horse and wagon carrying the bomb were blown to bits.

The solemn offices of J. P. Morgan & Co., probable target of the bomb, were a scene of twisted metal and debris. The company's chief clerk was killed by shattered glass.

Brown Brothers

Humor and crime make odd bedfellows. Yet occasionally a debonair crook arises who takes his arrest lightly and turns it into a brief, merry jape.

One such was Nicky Arnstein, husband of *Follies* star Fannie Brice. Charming, plausible, well-read, Arnstein had previously been a cardsharp on trans-Atlantic liners, where he was such fine company that many of his victims enjoyed being cheated by him. One wealthy traveler, warned of being hooked by Nicky, shrugged and said, "I don't give a damn. He's better company than anyone else aboard ship."

Nicky's existence was tranquil as long as he remained on the decks of luxury liners. But when he stepped ashore the clever touch seemed to fade. Weary of criss-crossing the Atlantic, he allowed himself to become involved in a clumsy swindle in New York. He was caught and sent to jail. Even there his outstanding qualities were recognized. He was appointed prison librarian.

Then Nicky met Fannie Brice, a rough-and-tumble girl from the Lower East Side. His easy manners and erudition quickly won her. In 1921 the two were married, after which Nicky devoted himself to the graceful life he understood so well. Then suddenly came word that he had been named as the mastermind of a series of holdups of Wall Street messengers carrying securities from one brokerage house to another. Fannie was outraged. "Mastermind!" she snorted. "Nick couldn't mastermind an electric light bulb into a socket."

Yet Nick was wanted by police. The man who carried the gun in the holdups had seen Rogues Gallery photos and unhesitatingly picked him out as the mysterious Mr. A who ran things from the safety of uptown. Nick learned all this through the underworld grapevine and took it on the lam ahead of police. Where he hid, nobody knew—not even Fannie. Nicky's lawyer was dashing Bill Fallon, immortalized by Gene Fowler in *The Great Mouthpiece*. In time, Fallon approached police with a set of terms for Nicky Arnstein's surrender. Nick would give himself up provided

Follies star Fannie Brice (RIGHT) awaited husband Nicky Arnstein at Police Headquarters after his arrest. A Rogues' Gallery file and a loyal friend of Fannie's complete the picture.

38. A CROOK WITH A SENSE OF HUMOR

131

he could walk up Headquarters' steps under his own steam; he must not have handcuffs clapped over sensitive wrists; food must be sent to his cell from an outside restaurant; he must be allowed to dress from his own fancy wardrobe. Nicky and Fallon had many friends among reporters and the story made page one of the newspapers. Police fumed at his arrogance, but they couldn't locate the fugitive themselves and had to agree.

The law should have known something was up when Nicky set the day of the annual Fifth Avenue police parade as his time of surrender. Un-suspecting cops massed for the great parade, leaving a few men at Headquarters to await Arn-stein. Nick had his own plans. He and Fallon, together with a New York *World* reporter, met far uptown and climbed into the rear of a chauf-feur-driven, top-down, town car. Then they were driven slowly downtown.

The timing was perfect. Just as the last platoon of the parade moved forward, the car with Arn-stein and Fallon arrived to follow it. Thus the Mayor, Police Commissioner, and other digni-taries on the reviewing stand suddenly found themselves doffing toppers and paying tribute to the criminal who had been on the much-publi-cized lam for the last few months. As the Com-missioner's apoplectic roars shattered the air, Arnstein gave a debonair wave. Then his car drove on to Headquarters.

Arnstein's humor-under-pressure takes on new dimension when it is realized that he was prob-ably innocent of the mastermind charge. For with the murder of Broadway gambler Arnold Roth-stein in 1928 (see page 169), evidence pointed to Rothstein as the Mr. A who masterminded the downtown holdups. After pulling several jobs under the mysterious Mr. A's direction, the down-town gang demanded to see their boss. Rothstein instructed a henchman to lead them to the win-dow of a fashionable restaurant where Nicky Arnstein habitually dined at a table by the win-dow. Arnstein was pointed out as Mr. A.

Nicky may or may not have been aware of all this. But he was found guilty of organizing the robberies and sentenced to the Federal pen. After serving his time, he faced life without Fannie. For she had learned that even in their moments of greatest happiness charming Nicky had played around with other women. Heartbroken Fannie was through.

Birds of a feather, Dapper Nick and his lawyer, Bill Fallon, the Great Mouthpiece, made a lark of lawlessness. Both liked to laugh at adversity, brighten life with whiskey, girls and song.

Whenever with a lady admirer, Roscoe "Fatty" Arbuckle seemed as amiable as when on the screen. Ranking just behind Chaplin as a comedian, he had been a poor little fat boy as a child.

United Press International Photo

39. A COMEDIAN'S LAST BIG PARTY

With the advent of the Twenties, the movie star made a spectacular appearance on the American scene. Frequently lifted to the peak of fame from the depths of poverty, he—or she—earned thousands of dollars a week at a time when the income tax was all but nonexistent.

Charles Chaplin, Mary Pickford, and Douglas Fairbanks were the famous names of this young, fabulous Hollywood. Right behind them was

Roscoe "Fatty" Arbuckle, aged 34. Born in Smith Corners, Kansas, Arbuckle came into the world weighing a walloping sixteen pounds. As a child, he looked the perfect fat boy, which caused his parents to shove him toward show business. Roscoe hardly went to school, absorbing his education from the rough backstage world of vaudeville. When films arrived, he was the ideal fat fellow for the Keystone Kops. Next he began producing his own comedies, and these earned him a place just behind Charlie Chaplin as the world's most cherished comedian. In 1921, Fatty Arbuckle signed a contract which would bring him $3,000,000 in three years—nearly $3,000 a day.

Fatty Arbuckle not only looked the average jolly fat man, but lived the part. He loved to laugh and spend money. He also liked to work and was both skillful and conscientious at the fine art of comedy. His hobby was drinking, and his 266-pound body absorbed liquor in prodigious quantities. His passion was girls. "If there weren't beautiful women in the world, I wouldn't want to be alive," he was fond of saying. His attitude toward the opposite sex often reflected his rough backstage upbringing. "All girls got the same round heels, no matter who they are," he reputedly told a friend who objected to his blunt approach to l'amour. Yet he was a top star and Hollywood had enough willing, ambitious girls to make this bluntness pay off.

One girl on whom Fatty appeared to make no impression was 25-year-old Virginia Rappe, whose face adorned the sheet music of "Let Me Call You Sweetheart." Her delicate beauty, rather than acting ability, had made her a leading lady in Hollywood films. Virginia Rappe was in love with a film director, but the man seemed in no hurry to marry her. Just before Labor Day, 1921, the director left without her for New York. Perhaps because she missed him Virginia agreed to accompany another couple on a Labor Day weekend trip to San Francisco. What she didn't know was that Arbuckle, whose eye was on her, had persuaded the couple to invite her.

Arbuckle drove to San Francisco on Saturday, accompanied by actor Lowell Sherman. They rode in Fatty's $25,000 Rolls Royce, equipped with built-in toilet in the back seat. Virginia made the trip with her friends. The two groups arrived at 2 A.M. but did not meet then. Virginia and her friends registered at the Palace Hotel. Arbuckle took a suite on the twelfth floor of the sedate St. Francis. Arraying his vast form in a dressing gown, he immediately began to guzzle Prohibition gin. Lowell Sherman went to sleep, which displeased Fatty, who sat up all night drinking. At 11 A.M. the next day, a gay group of San Francisco friends arrived for a party. Arbuckle, by now angry and sullen, woke Sherman and ordered him to join the fun. Then he phoned the

United Press International Photo

Arbuckle's inevitable movie role was the genial fat boy, a little backward mentally but jolly withal.

Palace and told Virginia's friends to bring her over.

What Arbuckle apparently had in mind was an orgy, and as time passed, at least two drunken girls obliged him by unbuttoning clothes to compare chest measurements. For once Fatty was not interested in such a display. His eyes were on Virginia Rappe, who sat drinking quietly. From time to time she complained of inability to get into the bathroom—it was always occupied. At last she got up and moved toward it. As she came close, Arbuckle took her arm and led her instead into the bedroom. Virginia did not protest—could she have been *that* drunk? Fatty closed and locked the door and for twenty minutes all was quiet, while the guests regarded each other knowingly. Then from behind the locked door came piercing screams and Virginia's cry, "I'm dying, he's killing me, I'm dying!"

Fatty Arbuckle was tried three times for Virginia Rappe's rape-death, the official theory being that he forced her into intercourse and ruptured her distended bladder by his weight. Arbuckle

134

denied all and declared—with some evidence—
that Virginia was not as pure as painted and had
really been interested in his advances. He recalled
the party through an alcoholic fog, as did other
guests. Confused testimony became hopelessly
tangled as Hollywood tried to salvage a $3,000,-

*Arbuckle's hours behind bars were few, but after
three sordid trials his career was finished. He died
ten years later, a broken man.*

000 star by passing out bribe-money. Witnesses
disappeared and memories blanked out with
extraordinary rapidity.

The first two trials resulted in hung juries. The
last was for acquittal, with the jury foreman stat-
ing, "We feel a great injustice has been done him."
This echoed a feeling in some quarters that, whatever his faults, Fatty Arbuckle had been the victim of a one-in-a-million freak accident. Cheered
by the verdict, his studio bosses decided his career
was saved and announced more Arbuckle pictures. But they had not taken the hinterlands into
consideration. From areas outside big cities came
thunderous protests and threats to boycott Arbuckle pictures, now and forever.

Fatty was finished. For ten years the fat man
wandered unhappily around the movie world,
directing a few pictures and begging for a chance
at a comeback. This seemed possible in 1933, but
precisely at that moment Fatty Arbuckle died of
a heart attack.

*The pretty face of Virginia Rappe adorned the
sheet music of "Let Me Call You Sweetheart."
Her distaste for Arbuckle may have cost her life.*

Where Fatty Arbuckle was crude, director William Desmond Taylor (ABOVE, with car and chauffeur) was smooth. But he too was a womanizer, and probably met death as a result.

Taylor looked the perfect stage Englishman, an appearance that turned out to be deceiving.

1922

40. HOLLYWOOD'S MYSTERIOUS MURDER

Even as Fatty Arbuckle was sweating through his ordeal in San Francisco, Hollywood came up with another murder. It was as subtle and sophisticated as the Arbuckle crime was crude.

The victim was William Desmond Taylor, English-born, forty-five, and handsome in a calm, aristocratic way. Taylor had begun acting in films in 1910. After a World War I stint in the Canadian army, he had returned to California to become the leading director for Famous Players-Lasky, which eventually became Paramount. Taylor made $100,000 a year, with his name flashing on the screen before some of the most popular films of the day. Fan magazines added to his glamour, carrying his by-line on articles which gave his bachelor views on actresses and women in general.

Taylor lived in a splendid Spanish-style home in an expensive residential colony opposite Westlake Park. His neighbors said women visited him at all hours of the day and night. Hollywood, which rated Fatty Arbuckle a lecher, called the suave Taylor a satyr. At the same time, he was a cultured chap who as early as 1922 was attempting to interest film-colony friends in the writings of Dr. Sigmund Freud.

Yet with all this good fortune, Taylor had pressing problems. One was a valet named Edward Sands. The year before, while the director traveled alone in Europe, Sands stepped into his master's shoes, forging checks, selling clothes,

United Press International Photo

A top director for Famous Players-Lasky, Taylor served apprenticeship as actor in early flicks.

smashing cars. On his return, Taylor fired the man, but it had been an expensive business. Since then, the director's home had been burgled twice. Taylor blamed Sands, but made no effort to locate or prosecute him.

A continuing problem was women, for girls who spent time with William Desmond Taylor dreamed of marrying the man. One was the piquant comedienne Mabel Normand, next to Mary Pickford the most popular actress in films. Miss Normand considered herself Taylor's fiancée, though others disputed this. Another who adored Taylor was 20-year-old Mary Miles Minter, who resembled Mary Pickford in her girlish curls, child-actress background, and air of total innocence. Miss Minter's mother also wanted to marry the urbane Taylor. Many, many others wrote him passionate avowals of love and left silken underthings in his bedroom as mementoes.

At 6 P.M. on February 1, 1922, Taylor seemed to be at loose ends. He phoned Mabel Normand, asking her to pay him a visit. Pert Mabel was weary after a hard day at the studio. She agreed to come over for a cocktail or two, but no more. When she arrived, Taylor dismissed his new butler-valet, Peavy. He and Mabel sipped and talked, with Mabel dropping peanut shells on the expensive rug. At 7:45 P.M. she went home, carrying a book by Freud. At 8:15 that evening, Mr. and Mrs. Douglas McLean, close neighbors, heard a noise. Looking out, they saw a man leaving the Taylor house. Later, Edna Purviance, another neighbor, ran over and rang the doorbell. Taylor's car was in the garage, but when no one answered the bell she decided he was entertaining a girl. At 7:30 the next morning, the valet Peavy reappeared to find his employer lying dead on his back on the living room floor. Even in death, Taylor looked completely at ease and the first doctor diagnosed the death as natural. But when the body was rolled over, two neat bullet holes showed in the back. . . .

The news blew Hollywood sky high. Mary Miles Minter's mother hurried around town looking for her daughter, who had been out suspiciously late the night before. When found, Miss Minter rushed to see Mabel Normand and the two compared notes behind a locked bathroom door for an interesting half hour. Red-hot letters from Mabel were found in the dead man's desk, and in his bedroom were handkerchiefs monogrammed MMM. Outside the back door lay a pile of cigarette butts, and police deduced that the killer stood there waiting for Mabel Normand to leave. But despite this, and the McLeans' sight of a departing man, officials suspected a woman.

Cleopatra in an early film, Mary Miles Minter had no career left after Taylor's murder. Investigation revealed her deep attachment to him and cast suspicion on her.

United Press International Photo

Star Mabel Normand, who had expected to become Mrs. Taylor, was spared the immediate consequences of the scandal.

Taylor's voluminous love correspondence included letters in code. In the one above, the symbols matched the letters of the alphabet.

But which? There were new beauties at every turn.

Next the case took a turn that might have been devised by an Agatha Christie or Edgar Wallace. Taylor, it turned out, was no Taylor. His real name was William Cunningham Deane-Tanner. Instead of being English, as he said, he was Irish. Deane-Tanner had been unusually close to his younger brother Denis, and the two had come to New York to open an antique shop. Both married, but were poor husbands who deserted their wives. When William began appearing in films under his new name, Denis played supporting roles. The police decided that the erring valet Sands had been brother Denis. But he couldn't be found—and never was!

There was more. Hollywood's pampered darlings had been experimenting with cocaine. Wallace Reid and Barbara Lamarr, both stars, soon died of the habit. Mabel Normand was trying the stuff, and Taylor had gone to Federal authorities to complain of the ease with which she obtained it. Perhaps the underworld had killed him for this. Or perhaps the murderer was in search of love letters with which to blackmail screen beauties. Peavy, the butler-valet, was a lisping homosexual, an odd type for a robust male like Taylor to have around. This opened up another road of investigation.

But always the search came back to the fair sex. Police reasoned that a jealous, vengeful woman must have shot Taylor from behind as he sat writing. The case was never solved, but left in its wake embarrassing revelations. Investigators found that Mary Miles Minter was thirty instead of twenty—she looked fifteen. This and the MMM's in Taylor's drawers ended her career. Mabel Normand escaped for the moment, but within a year made headlines when her chauffeur took a pot-shot at one of her admirers. Suspicion grew that the chauffeur was her lover, and madcap Mabel's acting days were over.

Two scandal-murders in six months put the movie industry in a state of shock, while the public viewed Hollywood as Sodom and Gomorrah. The Arbuckle case was bad enough. Taylor's murder had involved many of the most celebrated names in the film colony, revealed that some took dope. Industry leaders hastily got together and imported former Postmaster General Will H. Hays to serve, at $100,000 a year, as czar of movie morals and behavior. Hollywood had its scandals after that—but not as messy nor as close together.

138

41. THE CLERGYMAN AND THE CHOIR SINGER

Two young lovers in search of rustic privacy stumbled on the bodies stretched under a crabapple tree on De Russey's Lane, outside New Brunswick, New Jersey on September 17, 1922.

The dead man was dressed in a neat, dark suit, with a clerical collar. The woman, whose head rested in the crook of her companion's arm, wore a blue dress with lively red polka dots. The man's expensive Panama hat had been carefully placed over his face. Under it the eyeglasses had been set firmly on his nose, over closed eyes. The woman's face was covered by the end of a long woolen scarf. Her legs were crossed, with the skirt demurely pulled below her knees.

A robust diver, the Rev. Mr. Edward Wheeler Hall stayed young in heart while his wife grew older.

A choir singer, Eleanor Mills was the wife of the church sexton and had a sweet, though untrained voice.

139

Born an aristocrat and increasingly secluded after her marriage, Mrs. Hall rarely smiled in photographs but did in this one.

Between the bodies—scattered over them, some accounts say—were papers which turned out to be torrid love letters written in a woman's hand. Plainly the person or persons who committed the double crime had not fled in terror from the scene, but had stayed to arrange the corpses in this unusual manner. The most macabre touch of all was a dignified calling card propped against the soles of the dead man's upturned feet. It identified him as the Reverend Mr. Edward Wheeler Hall, pastor of St. John the Evangelist, most fashionable Episcopal church in New Brunswick.

His companion in death proved to be Mrs. Eleanor Mills, wife of the lowly sexton-janitor of the church. At forty-one, Hall was still boyish looking and popular with his large flock. Mrs. Mills, thirty-four, was mildly pretty, a voracious reader, and by far the sweetest singer in the church choir. For several years these two had been having a love affair, but both Hall's wife and Mrs. Mills' husband appeared unaware of it.

From a distance, the two carefully arranged bodies seemed more asleep than dead. But they were dead. The Reverend Mr. Hall had been killed—these details emerged later—by a single .32 bullet through the head. Mrs. Mills had been killed by a triangle of shots in the forehead. Her throat had also been cut, nearly severing the head. As a last grisly act, her tongue, larynx, and upper windpipe—the sweet singer's entire voice box—had been sliced out.

The Hall-Mills case stands forth as an example of two clichés of crime. One is that police do bungle. No autopsy was made on the bodies, no coroner's inquest held. Instead of performing these official acts immediately, the local law began a fight over whether Somerset or Middlesex County had jurisdiction. While the intramural battle waged, a thousand people a day rampaged over De Russey's Lane, trampling clues. The crabapple tree vanished, torn to bits by souvenir hunters. In a nearby farmhouse a so-called museum of the crime was set up. For fifty cents, rubbernecks could view remaining bits of the tree and other juicy items.

The second cliché is the behavior of a town when one of its first families becomes involved in murder. The Reverend Mr. Hall had married Frances Carpender Stevens, seven years his senior and daughter of an old and respected New Brunswick family. The marriage appeared satisfactory on the surface, though Hall continued young and bouncy while his wife—who was forty-eight in 1922—retired into a kind of somber respectability.

One of Mrs. Hall's problems was her swarthy, bushy-haired brother Willie Stevens, who at times seemed halfwitted, at others, super-smart. Willie Stevens loved to hang around the local firehouse pretending to be a fireman. At the same time, he had made himself an expert in botany, metallurgy, and entomology. Willie Stevens could make foolish remarks and pithy ones. New Brunswick didn't know what to make of him. Neither did the ninety-odd New York reporters

140

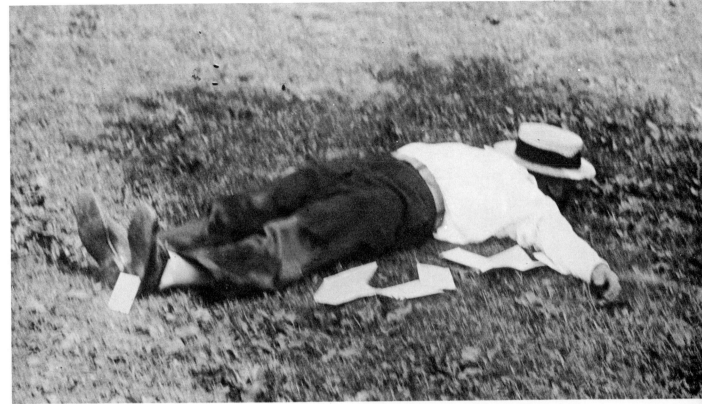

The position of Hall's body when found was simulated by a detective. Hall's calling card had been propped at his feet and love letters written by Mrs. Mills strewn by his side.

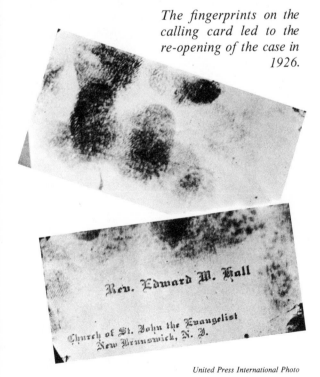

The fingerprints on the calling card led to the re-opening of the case in 1926.

who descended on the town immediately after the double murder.

Mrs. Hall had another brother named Henry Stevens, who looked so much the aristocratic clubman that gossip called Willie Stevens his father's illegitimate offspring by a mulatto. Henry Stevens was an expert shot, and inevitably suspicion arose that Mrs. Hall, Willie, and Henry had tracked the lovers to De Russey's Lane, perhaps discovering them in an intimate act. The possibility was upheld by a bizarre figure. This was Mrs. Jane Gibson who ran a pig farm near De Russey's Lane and was instantly dubbed the Pig Woman by the press. She claimed that at ten-thirty on the night of September 17, 1922, she had been out chasing a prowler. She saw and heard a group of people arguing on De Russey's Lane. A woman screamed and cried out, "Oh my! Oh my! Oh my!" Then came shots.

Solution of the crime was slowed both by police bungling and by the enormous prestige of the Stevens family. Mrs. Hall did not use overt pressure—social importance did it for her. Police

141

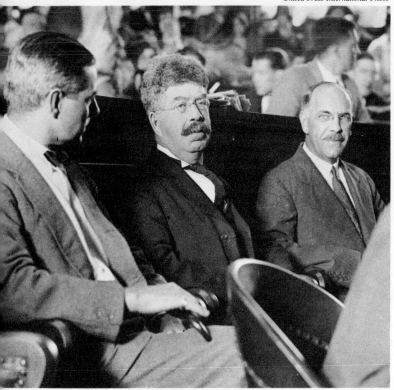

questioned her with extreme deference. Reporters from New York were not allowed into her presence, which drove them to concentrate on Mrs. Mills' shambling husband and her jazzy flapper daughter. When at last a Grand Jury of top citizens convened, Mrs. Hall was not even called before it.

The Grand Jury refused to act further, thereby closing the case. This left Mrs. Hall free to take an extended trip to Europe, while Willie Stevens stayed home to don a red shirt and hang around his beloved firehouse. In 1922, the sensational Hall-Mills murder seemed to have ended without further sensation.

Four years later, at midnight on the night of July 17, 1926, a cordon of police was dramatically thrown around the imposing Hall residence. Mrs. Hall, preparing for bed, was summoned downstairs and arrested for murder. So were her brothers, swarthy Willie and gentlemanly Henry. Directing the police officers was Philip Payne, managing editor of the tabloid New York *Mirror*.

Willie Stevens, a cheery enigma, seemed never more alert than during the trial. He had the reputation of being both half-wit and smart cooky.

The star witness, Mrs. Jane Gibson was wheeled into court on a stretcher and went out screaming accusations at Mrs. Hall.

Payne had got hold of the calling card found at the Reverend Mr. Hall's feet, then produced a fingerprint expert who swore the card showed the blurred prints of Willie Stevens. With this he persuaded Governor A. Harry Moore to reopen the unsolved mystery.

The New York *Daily News* and the New York *Graphic,* tabloids both, also fanned the flames of sensationalism in the case. So did every other newspaper in the country, including the New York *Times.* This time Mrs. Hall and her brothers were brought to trial, and newspapers instantly dubbed it the Trial of the Century. Beginning on November 3rd it ran for twenty-two sensation-soaked days, while reporters like Damon Runyon filed twelve million words through a giant switchboard which had been built for the Dempsey-Tunney championship fight in Philadelphia.

The prosecutor selected by Governor Moore was Alexander Simpson, small as a jockey, dressy as a tout. He relied heavily on the fingerprints on the calling card and the evidence of Mrs. Jane Gibson, the Pig Woman.

In the courtroom Mrs. Hall looked and acted exactly like the wealthy widow she was. Willie Stevens, popeyed and bushy-haired, enjoyed every moment of his notoriety. Henry Stevens was dignity itself. As days of testimony passed one fact became abundantly clear. Edward Wheeler Hall and Eleanor Mills had loved each other deeply, and it was part of Mrs. Hall's ordeal to sit through a reading of their passionate love letters. Yet on the witness stand the formidable widow insisted she had known nothing of the love affair. Cross-examination by the terrier-like Simpson failed to shake her.

Nor did the peppery little prosecutor score with Willie Stevens, widely believed to be half-witted. Willie's ingenuous answers were so friendly and shrewd that Simpson repeatedly fell back in confusion. Through the early days of the trial Mrs. Gibson, the Pig Woman, waited in the corridor to testify. Suddenly she was faced there by her crone-like mother, who called her a congenital liar and delivered such a tongue-lashing that the hefty Pig Woman collapsed. Rushed to a hospital, she was found to have cancer.

Yet she testified. Dramatically wheeled into court on a hospital bed, she croaked out the story of mounting her mule Jenny to ride through De Russey's Lane. Time had sharpened her memory and the sick woman introduced new details into her account of seeing a Dodge sedan—the Halls

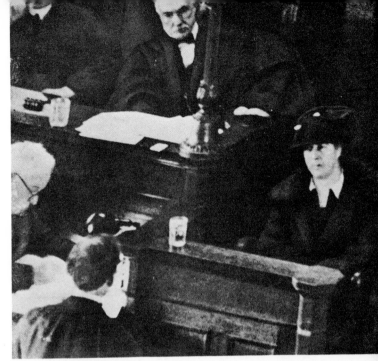

True to her upbringing, Mrs. Hall was poised on the stand as she denied even knowing of the love affair.

had one—and a middle-aged woman with a man, who she thought might have been Willie. She heard a woman's voice demand, "Explain these letters!" Next came terrible screams and shots. Finally, the Pig Woman said, she had seen Mrs. Hall kneeling prayerfully on the ground, bidding farewell to her dead husband. As she was being wheeled out of the courtroom, she rose up on an elbow to screech at Mrs. Hall, "I told the truth, so help me God! And *you* know it, *you* know it, *you* know it!"

Mrs. Gibson scored some telling points. Testimony about Willie's fingerprints on the calling card was also strong. But the jury was swayed by other matters. Before the trial, Alexander Simpson, a native of Jersey City, called residents of Somerset County country bumpkins, and made other slighting remarks. Resentment over this still bubbled high, while Simpson's flamboyant courtroom manner acted as salt in the open wound. It took six hours for the Somerset County jury to bring in a verdict of not guilty.

Mrs. Hall, exonerated at last, promptly sued the New York *Mirror* for $3,000,000. The suit was settled out of court for an unspecified amount, reputedly large.

143

42. DEATH OF A BUTTERFLY

Dot King, sob sisters said, was another good girl gone wrong. Tabloids named her the Broadway Butterfly and blazoned her story in headlines, calling it a tragedy of the Prohibition Twenties.

Born Dorothy Keenan to an uptown Irish slum family in New York City, she was an attractive child who turned into an exceedingly pretty girl. Her hair was natural-blonde, eyes sparkling blue, smile demure. Around her, as she grew up, were the stock figures of romance. Her hardworking father was unsympathetic, impatiently anticipating his daughter's first mistake. Her mother, proud and adoring, protected her from the suspicious father. An older sister, not so pretty, married young and promptly began producing children. Two older brothers protected the kid sister as long as she craved protection, but turned hostile and resentful when she no longer did. In her mid-teens Dorothy began welcoming the attention of boys. Next she discovered that older men were anxious for her company and would take her to gay, expensive places. She began staying out late, giving her father good reason to throw her out.

Dorothy Keenan moved downtown, changed her name to Dot King, and got a job as a model in a Fifth Avenue dress shop. The year was 1915, when the introduction of jazz turned Broadway into a street of cabarets where couples emulated Vernon and Irene Castle by dancing the Bunny Hug and Turkey Trot. Dot King, footloose, young, and lovely, became a conspicuous part of the frivolity.

She remained so during the hectic days of World War I. When Broadway night life went underground with Prohibition, Dot went with it, becoming a hostess in a speakeasy. By some accounts she was a *Follies* girl, but this is unlikely. She had no talent, nor was she the statuesque type of beauty favored by Florenz Ziegfeld for show girls. Dot was small and peppy, epitome of the short-skirted flapper just coming into vogue. She was a playgirl at heart, and followed

Dot King and Alberto Guimares looked happy, but were playing out the sad saga of a girl who loves a bum. Guimares lived on Dot's money, and gave her only trouble in return.

United Press International Photo

the pattern of the type by finding an elderly protector who set her up in an apartment at 144 West 57th Street, near Carnegie Hall.

He gave her an allowance, paid the rent, the bills, hired her a maid, and showered her with jewelry—$30,000 worth, in all. Dot knew him only as Mr. Marshall, a rich banker from Boston. He visited her about twice a week, making a production of it. First his bodyguard named Walter knocked at the door. Walter investigated the apartment to make sure Dot was alone. After that, Marshall entered and passed the night.

Marshall's twice-weekly visits left Dot ample time to roam the speakeasy world. Here she met a smooth, side-burned Latin named Alberto Santos Guimares who lived by petty swindling and the exploitation of women. Dot fell madly in love with him. From her allowance she gave him money and bought him clothes, in return for which he regularly beat her up. This seemed right to Dot. Like many girls living in so-called sin, she harbored a masochistic desire to be punished.

Dot was found dead in bed by her maid at noon on March 15, 1923. She had been killed by chloroform, applied by such rough hands that scratches showed around her nose and eyes. The chloroform bottle, with stopper in, lay under the bed. A wad of chloroform-soaked cotton was on the pillow near Dot's blonde head. The bedroom had been ransacked as if the killers (or killer) had been searching for something. Whether or not it was found, the intruders had carried off as many of Dot's jewels and clothes as could be taken in their arms.

Good-hearted Dot had reconciled with her family and with Marshall's money even bought one of her brothers a taxicab. The family also knew of Guimares' brutal beatings and told police. This made the Latin lover seem the prime suspect, but he had an alibi. On the murder night he had been two-timing Dot, oozing his charm over socialite Mrs. Aurelia Dreyfus. She backed this up. Police turned to interrogating the maid and elevator boys, and learned about Mr. Marshall. No banker of that name lived in Boston. Police released a letter to Dot in Marshall's handwriting which ended, "I kiss your pretty pink toes." Following this a circumspect phone call to headquarters identified Marshall as J. Kearsley Mitchell, son-in-law of E. T. Stotesbury, the most formidable millionaire on Philadelphia's Main Line. Mitchell told police he had taken Dot

A flapper in furs, Dot King was too pretty for her own good. Born into a poor New York family, she gravitated to the bright lights and was a belle of the speakeasy era.

to dinner the night before the murder and returned with her about midnight. He departed about 2:30 A.M. No one had seen him leave at that time, or any other. Out of consideration for the elevator boy, he said, he had walked down stairs. Like Guimares, he was let go.

Eventually police fell back on the convenient theory that Dot was the victim of robbers. Two men, it was reasoned, followed Mitchell and the

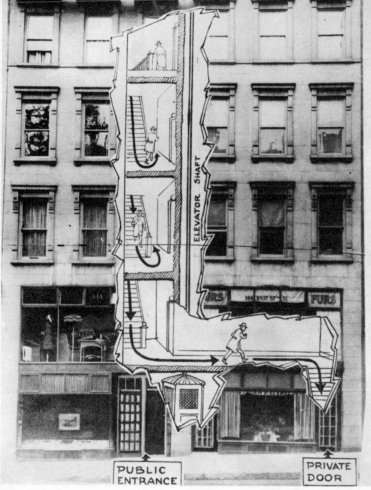

expensively dressed young girl home from the restaurant. After waiting for Mitchell to leave, they entered Dot's apartment intending to use the chloroform to knock her out while stealing her jewelry. Using too much chloroform, they killed her. At this, they panicked, grabbed everything in sight, and ran.

But if two ordinary robbers killed Dot King, police never found them. Or were the men in search of little-pink-toes letters from Marshall? In which case they were probably hired by Guimares, who planned to blackmail the Philadelphia aristocrat.

A year later Guimares and Mrs. Dreyfus stood on the balcony of her Washington hotel suite. Somehow she fell, jumped, or was pushed to her death. Among her effects was an affidavit swearing she had perjured herself in supporting Guimares' alibi for Dot's murder. Since the lady gave no further details, police had nothing specific to work on. Nor could they prove the slippery Latin had pushed Mrs. Dreyfus from the balcony.

Guimares lived on, a petty crook and womanizer, until 1953, when he died. He made no deathbed confession. If the murder of Dot King—or any fond recollections of the lively girl—ever bothered him, he showed no signs of it.

The man, or men, who killed Dot King had a choice of exits, one hidden from elevator operator's sight. The murderer was never found, though cops tried hard to trap Guimares.

At Atlantic City, Dot and Guimares posed on one of their many trips together. Their travels were paid for by money given Dot by a sugar daddy.

The Teapot Dome oil preserve got its name from this curious rock formation in Wyoming. The area held vast national oil reserves which Interior Secretary Albert Fall leased to oil-baron friends.

1923

43. TEAPOT DOME

The inside story of the Harding Administration resembles a Grade-B thriller.

Even the main character was contrived, for Warren G. Harding, President of the United States, lacked ability for the high post. Rather, he possessed a benevolent, fatherly handsomeness which added up to the perfect Presidential image. This was recognized as early as 1900 by an ambitious Ohio politician named Harry Daugherty when he saw Harding at a political meeting. "Gee, what a President he'd make," Daugherty thought, and set about making him one.

At first the easygoing Harding was reluctant to leave the job of publisher-editor of the Marion, Ohio, *Star*. Mrs. Harding joined with Daugherty

and the two persuaded him to enter Ohio politics. In 1915 he was elected to the U.S. Senate, where he served without distinction. In 1920, in a smoke-filled room in Chicago, he was given the Republican nomination for President. By then, Mrs. Harding feared what she had wrought. "I can see but one word written above his head if they make him President," she said, "and that word is Tragedy."

Tragedy commenced as soon as Harding took office. Harry Daugherty had remained his trusted adviser through the years and as a reward the President appointed him U.S. Attorney General and patronage dispenser. Like any cheap politician who had won a local election, Daugherty brought his cronies with him to Washington. The

Ohio Gang, as the group was quickly called, let it be known they were in the nation's capital solely to make money. Everything had a price. Judgeships, public lands, the newly lucrative job of Prohibition agent—all these and more were up for sale.

A so-called "House on 16th Street" became the headquarters for bribery and mysterious pay-offs. A "Little Green House on H Street" offered bathtub gin, girls, and poker games which corrupted those slow to play the game. Both estab-

Cabinet. His New Mexico ranch was run-down, his properties mortgaged. Altogether, Fall was about $100,000 in the hole. His Department had jurisdiction over rich oil lands held in reserve in case of war, and Fall allowed himself to be persuaded that these reserves were being drained of oil by adjacent commercial operations. He declared it in the national interest to lease the dormant fields at Teapot Dome, Wyo., and Elk Hills, Calif., to private companies. Without asking for bids, he signed contracts with Edward

Attorney General Harry Daugherty (ABOVE), *groomed Warren G. Harding for the Presidency. After election Daugherty brought the Ohio Gang of accomplished grafters to Washington. Fall may have been influenced by the activities of the Attorney General.*

lishments were operated by the Attorney General through his Ohio henchman, Jess Smith. Harding knew of them but now he feared his old friend Daugherty. Harding had fathered an illegitimate child and Daugherty was one who knew all the details. Daugherty had also persuaded the President to invest in the stock market and loaned him the money to do it. Harding's stocks fell, so in addition he owed money to Daugherty.

Washington seemed permeated by corruption. Cabinet members like Charles Evans Hughes and Herbert Hoover remained untempted, but few others could resist. One who succumbed was Secretary of the Interior Albert B. Fall. A one-time oil man, he had fallen on unhappy days before a near-miraculous appointment to the

L. Doheny and Harry B. Sinclair, oil world millionaires. These two men expected to make at least $100,000,000 from the leases, so it is hardly surprising that Doheny slipped Fall $100,000 in cash, while Sinclair saw to it he got $260,000 in Liberty Bonds.

Having neatly feathered his own nest, Fall turned to viewing the Washington scene. There was much to look at, for the Ohio Gang was plundering so boldly that exposure grew inevitable. Charles R. Forbes, head of the Veterans' Bureau and a Harding crony, was trapped accepting kickbacks from contractors picked to build new veterans hospitals. Rumors of $200,000,000 graft in the whole Veterans program followed, as Forbes went to jail. Then Jess Smith, Daugh-

Fall (LEFT) poses with Harry Sinclair, one of the millionaires to whom he leased Teapot Dome. Government cases against Fall and friends failed until he was tried alone in 1929 and convicted.

erty's bagman, suffered qualms of conscience and killed himself—or was he killed to prevent him from talking? Daugherty's house of corruption was crumbling fast and no one knew this better than the President. In office only two years and five months, he was already a broken—or breaking—man. To get away from it all the President entrained on a supposedly triumphal trip to Alaska in June 1923. In San Francisco, on the return, he died of a heart attack. Some say his wife poisoned him, but this lurid charge has never been substantiated.

Even with Harding alive, Senators LaFollette of Wisconsin and Walsh of Montana had attempted to expose the Washington corruption. With Harding dead, the man they wanted to get

was Daugherty. But if the Attorney General had been crude in permitting graft, he had carefully obscured his own participation. On trial for accepting $400,000 in bribes in an Alien Property Custodian case, he was freed by a jury which deliberated sixty-six hours.

For a moment it seemed that no high member of the Harding Administration would be brought to book. Then LaFollette remembered a letter from a Wyoming oilman asking how the government's Teapot Dome oil lands could be leased to Doheny and Sinclair. Secretary Fall had brushed this off at the time, as had Harding. Senator Walsh was now head of the Senate Subcommittee on Public Lands. He and LaFollette began digging into the leases. They became convinced that

149

Fall had accepted bribe money. One reason was the great improvements the ex-Secretary made in his New Mexico ranch.

The prosecution of Albert Fall ran through almost ten years of complicated investigation. The Department of Justice focused at first on the $100,000 cash bribe, since the $260,000 Liberty Bond payment was harder to unravel. The ex-Secretary, ruddy and vigorous, told a tale of borrowing $100,000 from the eccentric millionaire, Edward B. McLean. The unpredictable McLean denied it, which forced Fall to admit the money had been sent to him by Doheny in a little black bag. On the witness stand at the first Fall-Doheny trial, Doheny told a heart-rending story of two boys starting out together in life. One (Doheny) struck it rich in oil. The other (Fall) was dogged by bad luck. "Why shouldn't I lend him $100,000 and tear his name off the note?" Doheny demanded. "He was an old friend and to me the money was no more than twenty-five or thirty dollars would be to the average man." Later he called the $100,000 "a mere bagatelle." The national jaw dropped.

The Government lost its laboriously prepared cases against Fall-Doheny and Fall-Sinclair, though Sinclair went to jail for nine months for contempt of court. But the Justice Department tenaciously kept after Albert B. Fall. In 1929, he was tried alone. By now he was a frail and wispy old man who had to be pushed in and out of court in a wheel chair. This time the jury found him guilty of bribery charges, sentencing him to a year in jail and a fine of $100,000. Lacking the money, Fall signed a pauper's oath. Government doctors agreed with his personal physician that Fall had tuberculosis. As a special concession he was confined to the New Mexico State Penitentiary, to be near his family and breathe compatible air. Fall was carried into the prison on a stretcher, looking "pale to the point of ashiness." Nevertheless, he served his sentence and lived on—an invalid taken care of by his family—until 1944.

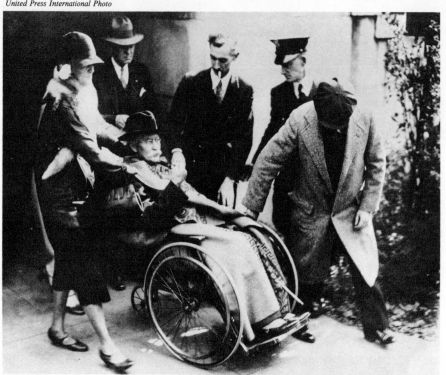

Eight long trials reduced Fall to a shattered figure wheeled into court. Millionaire Edward Doheny admitted giving Fall $100,000, called the sum "mere bagatelle."

44. LEOPOLD-LOEB

Telling their terrible story to the police, Nathan Leopold (LEFT) and Richard Loeb looked like the wealthy youths both of them were. The trial of the emotionally warped pair brought psychiatry into the courtroom.

Nathan Leopold, 19 and a Phi Beta Kappa, was the youngest student ever to graduate from the University of Chicago. Richard Loeb, 18, was the youngest ever to receive a diploma from the University of Michigan. These two, sons of rich, indulgent parents, lived close to each other in the wealthy Kenwood section of Chicago. Together they committed a super-sensational crime which newspapers quickly dubbed the Thrill Killing.

Leopold was brilliant, Loeb only clever. Yet Loeb, whose father was a Sears, Roebuck vice-president, was the dominant member of the duo. Clean-cut and unusually handsome, he detested the good looks which made him seem to possess the upstanding virtues of an All-American Boy. To prove to himself that he was not what the world thought him, Dickie Loeb began stealing. He stole so much without detection that he began to think of himself as a Superman.

Nathan Leopold, slight, stooped, near-sighted, was "Babe" to his friends. He adored handsome Dickie and offered to assume slave status—do anything Loeb ever ordered him to do. The thought of another human under his complete dominance appealed to Loeb's mind, already nursing delusions of grandeur. For more than four years, and through many quarrels, the strange tie persisted. Now, in the spring of 1924, the two teetered on the verge of separation, for Leopold planned to go to the Harvard Law School in the fall. Loeb decided it was now or never to prove his superiority to the rest of mankind by committing, with his worshipful slave, the Perfect Crime.

Leopold agreed, since by the pact he had to. The two decided to kill first. Then, to increase danger and excitement, pretend the crime was a kidnaping and collect ransom. For a time they considered Loeb's kid brother as the victim. Next they chose a pupil at the nearby Harvard School for Boys. On the afternoon of May 21, 1924, the two waited for him in a rented car outside the school, but the boy fooled them by going home early. Along came Bobby Franks, fourteen, a distant cousin of Loeb's. The pair offered to drive him home. Bobby, sensing danger, hesitated. The boy was a tennis player and Loeb hastily mentioned something about a new tennis racket. At this, Bobby Franks got in.

The car drove only a few blocks before Loeb crushed a gag into Bobby's mouth and brought a cold chisel down four times on the boy's bare

United Press International Photo

Bobby Franks, neighbor and cousin of Loeb's, accidentally walked into the murder plan.

head. Blood spurted, and Bobby slumped. Leopold, who was driving, turned for a quick look, "Oh, God," he mumbled, "I didn't know it would be like this." Loeb hauled Bobby to the floor of the rear seat and hit him three times more. Then he wrapped the boy's body in a lap robe. The pair drove for twenty miles through the teeming city while Bobby Franks bled to death in the rear of the car. At one point, feeling hungry, they jumped out for a snack.

152

Leopold's glasses, found near the body, first implicated the pair.

When darkness came, the young murderers drove to a desolate stretch along the Pennsylvania Railroad tracks. Before the crime, the two had labored over what were considered foolproof plans. Accordingly, they now carried the body to a culvert and stripped off the clothing. After pouring disfiguring acid over the face, they pushed the body into a drain-pipe. Leaving the scene, they again felt hungry and stopped to devour a full meal. Next stop was Loeb's house, where Bobby's clothes were burned in the furnace. After this, they drove to Leopold's, burying Bobby's belt buckle, the lap robe, and other items en route.

To kill time, they played cards until midnight. Now came the first step in the elaborate ransom plan. Phoning the Franks' home, they talked to Bobby's father. "Your son has been kidnaped," a deep voice told him. "He is safe. Don't worry. Instructions will follow."

In the morning a workman passing the Pennsylvania tracks saw a bare foot sticking out of the drain-pipe. By the time the perpetrators of the Perfect Crime telephoned Mr. Franks to give instructions about the first ransom payment, Bobby Franks was known to be dead.

Police swarmed through the Kenwood section, and no one seemed more anxious to help than handsome Dickie Loeb. As a neighbor and cousin of the victim, he attached himself to detectives, offering helpful suggestions in what he considered a clumsy investigation. Clumsy or not, police found a pair of horn-rimmed spectacles near the drain. Within eight days these were identified as Nathan Leopold's. He offered the explanation that he had recently been bird-watching in the area and lost his glasses then. As to the murder day, he declared that he and Loeb had passed it driving in the family touring car. The Leopold chauffeur, who had no love for the arrogant youths, contradicted him. Loeb, the would-be Superman, cracked first under stepped-up police interrogation. He called Leopold the killer. Told of this, Leopold snarled back a denial. Brought face to face, Loeb made peace by saying, "We're both in for the same ride, Babe, so we might as well ride together." Both then confessed.

Meanwhile, their wealthy families were beating on the door of Clarence Darrow, who as a criminal lawyer had already saved 102 accused murderers. No less than the rest of the world, Darrow was sickened by the pointless viciousness of the Thrill Killers. At the same time he hated capital punishment. "While the State tries Leopold and Loeb," he decided, "I will try capital punishment."

Darrow knew he could never win acquittal for the pair, and instructed them to plead guilty. Up to this point, insanity of one sort or another had been the usual plea in murder cases. Darrow determined to picture his clients as mentally ill rather than insane. To support this, he called in a small army of psychiatrists. Though brilliant mentally, Darrow declared, the two pampered youths were fixated at the emotional age of seven.

State Prosecutor Robert Crowe questioned Leopold as the youth re-took the driver's seat in the murder vehicle.

United Press International Photo

Sentenced to life plus ninety-nine years, Leopold and Loeb entered Joliet prison.

This plea may have marked a legal-psychiatric milestone, but it did not overly impress Judge Claverly, who heard the case without a jury. After sentencing the pair to life imprisonment, plus 99 years for kidnaping, he pointedly went on, "I do this not because they are abnormal or because they pleaded guilty, but because they are under age." Still, it was deemed a legal victory for Darrow.

Leopold and Loeb were hustled to Joliet Penitentiary, where Loeb was stabbed to death twelve years later in a sexual assault on another prisoner. Leopold, his prison record exemplary, was paroled in 1958. He went to Puerto Rico as a researcher in medicine, and there he married. In 1963, five years after parole, he automatically received complete freedom.

Wide World Photos, Inc.

With a wife and a new life, Leopold does medical research in Puerto Rico, having earned parole for being an exemplary prisoner. He met his wife there.

154

1924
45. TWO GENTLEMEN ROBBERS

Though in more than out of jail, Gerald Chapman was a master criminal to America of the Roaring Twenties. Above, during one of his many arrests.

America's much-headlined master criminal of the Twenties learned his lessons from a European criminal of the same stripe.

The American was Gerald Chapman, born Chartres, son of Irish-American parents. Raised in Brooklyn, he devoted youthful energies to petty crime. Between 1907, the year of his first arrest, and 1920, when he reached thirty, Chapman spent most of his time in prison for uninspired tries at robbery and jewel theft. Sentenced to New York's Auburn Prison, he had the good fortune—he thought—to be placed in a cell with the hardened criminal George "Dutch" Anderson. Though Anderson didn't look it, he was a true, if twisted, gentleman. Born Ivan Dahl von Teller in Denmark, he was the incorrigible son of a wealthy family. Dutch Anderson had been so well educated at Heidelberg and at Upsala in Sweden that he spoke five languages.

Through long prison days and nights, Anderson talked while Chapman listened. By the time

Chapman's accomplice, Danish-born "Dutch" Anderson had many disguises in which to hide his homeliness. Anderson's inspiration made Chapman a big-time crook.

his sentence ended, the American had a smattering of general knowledge and a man-of-the-world gloss, though inwardly he had not changed. He marked time until Anderson's release, then the two went to the Midwest, where they pulled off several lucrative jobs. Back in New York, they took a smart apartment on Gramercy Park. In classy new clothes, they posed as idle men of wealth.

The two were indeed paradoxical. Dutch Anderson, the gent, always looked like a homely thug. Chapman, who was a cheap crook, looked every inch the gentleman. Slight, with receding hair, unusually high cheekbones, and brooding eyes, he had the cultured air of a college president or a man who lived comfortably on income. Anderson's talk of good food and cigars had aroused in Chapman a taste for the finer things in life. On occasion he stepped out in monocle and spats, carrying a cane.

As high-echelon crooks the fancy pair found themselves living a long distance from pay dirt. To get funds, they periodically dropped the rich-man guise to mingle with underworld pals from Auburn and other prisons. One of these was a petty crook named Charles Loeber, who had hit on the idea of robbing one of the unguarded mail trucks which nightly carried mail from the Wall Street area to the Main Post Office. In the trucks was registered mail containing bonds, money orders, and securities amounting to millions. "The job's too big for me," Loeber said, "but maybe the three of us . . ."

Chapman and Anderson instantly ceased being playboys. With Loeber, they hung around the Park Row Post Office, making friends with the staff, studying layout, schedules, and types of mail. On the night of October 24, 1921, the three were ready. In a stolen Cleveland, they trailed the mail truck driven by Frank Havernack up a deserted Broadway. Suddenly the Cleveland crowded the truck to the curb, allowing the agile

Chapman to make a flying leap to Havernack's side. The driver stopped his truck and, on orders, opened the back door. The three robbers pushed him inside and climbed in after. Quickly they found five sacks of registered mail hidden under thirty-three regular pouches. After tying a laundry sack over Havernack's head, they fled. The sacks of registered mail were worth $1,454,129, the largest haul in the country to date.

In the green car the trio sped to Ronkonkoma, Long Island, where they stopped to make the dismal discovery that the pouches contained only $27,000 in cash. True, the more-than-a-million in bonds and money orders could be converted to cash, but this was a complicated business requiring payments as high as forty cents on the dollar to underworld fences. Still, it had to be done. Chapman and Anderson traveled to Muncie, Indiana, putting up at the farm of a friend named Ben Hance. After disposing of $100,000 in bonds, they returned to the high life of Gramercy Park. New York newspapers were still full of the daring robbery, but this did not inhibit the pair. They began spending $1,000 a day on cars, girls, and roadhouse gaiety.

Charles Loeber was their butler-chauffeur—and weak spot. With neither the brains nor patience to cash his share of the bonds out of town,

Chapman and Anderson won fame by robbing this mail truck, wresting over a million dollars worth of registered mail from driver Frank Havernack (INSET).

156

he tried in New York. This led detectives to the trio. Loeber quickly turned on his pals and offered to testify against them. His evidence got the two master criminals twenty-five years each in Atlanta.

While being held in New York, Chapman escaped and made his way to a ledge seventy-five feet above street level. It was a foolish try, since he couldn't reach the ground, but newspapers made much of the exciting moment and began turning him into a combination Raffles, Jimmy Valentine, and Jesse James. His ascetic looks added much to the myth. Thousands of pictures were taken of him in police stations and prison cells. In all, he seemed to be a gentleman taking his ease.

Chapman got additional headlines by twice escaping from Atlanta. After gargling a disinfectant he was committed to the prison hospital for a sore throat. Rising from his bed, he overpowered a guard and sawed his way through steel bars, then slid to the ground on a rope of knotted sheets. Two days later he was caught after being shot three times. Now he *needed* a hospital, but once again the nervy felon escaped by a rope of sheets. This time he got away and reached the Ben Hance farm in Indiana. Meantime, Dutch Anderson dug a tunnel under the prison wall and escaped. He joined Chapman at Muncie.

The two now evolved a plan of living in the Midwest while committing crimes in the East. The experience with Loeber should have taught the masterminds, but it didn't. Local tip-off men were necessary and in Connecticut they recruited one Walter Shean. Soon police in New Britain shot it out with two men attempting a daylight holdup of a department store. One policeman was killed, Walter Shean captured. Like any crime-struck kid, he boasted, "My pal was Gerald Chapman."

The nation reeled. A million-dollar mail robbery and three daredevil escapes had made Chapman a living legend. It was unthinkable that such a man would sink to small-time holdups and cop killing. When Chapman was captured in Muncie and transported to Hartford, the nation waited eagerly for him to escape again. He didn't. At a sensational trial, Walter Shean accused Chapman of killing the policeman, and natives of New Britain put him on the scene. Chapman in turn, swore he had only loaned his car to Shean. The verdict was guilty, and more than ever newspaper readers anticipated a break-

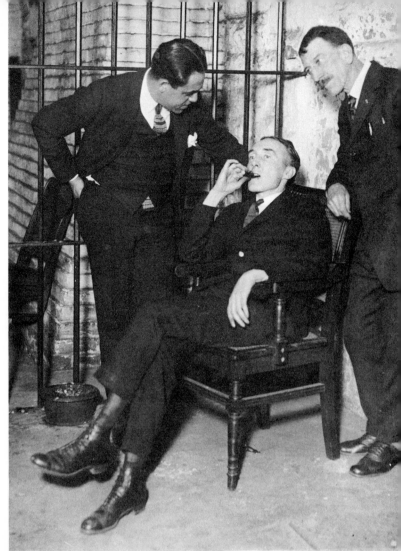

United Press International Photo

Chapman looked so much the gentleman that even behind bars men proudly posed with him. Here, with cigar and convenient spittoon, he awaits hanging for murder.

out. But Gerald Chapman seemed to have lost his fire. "Death itself isn't dreadful," he told a reporter, "but hanging seems an awkward way of entering the adventure." He was hanged on April 5, 1926.

It drove his mentor, Dutch Anderson, berserk. Rampaging the country, he tried to wreak personal vengeance on everyone who contributed to Chapman's downfall. He murdered the Indiana farmer Ben Hance and his wife in the mistaken belief that they had turned Chapman in. He set fire to the garage from which Chapman stole his getaway car. He tried to kill Walter Shean in jail, but couldn't reach him. In Muskegon, Mich., a cop finally recognized the European master criminal. The two men fired simultaneously, killing each other.

Suddenly Prohibition-era gangsters had seized control of Chicago. Scarface Al Capone, young war veteran, was now top man.

1926

46.

GANGLAND REIGNED SUPREME

As he walked toward the famous Chicago restaurant that bore his name, Big John Colosimo was a happy man. Only five days before this 49-year-old overlord of vice and gambling on the Windy City's South Side had married a lovely Australian girl whom he first saw singing in a local opera house. Conquest of the songbird had been a difficult business, involving the shedding of a wife, placating the Catholic Church, and enduring much gossip. Big John had survived all this and at last his world was bright.

Then suddenly it was pitch dark, for as he stepped into the vestibule of his restaurant a burst of fire from the cloakroom cut him down. . . .

This was the first of the Prohibition murders which tore Chicago apart and earned the city its reputation as the most lawless area in the modern world. Big John Colosimo had been among the first to see the enormous possibilities for illegal profit in the Eighteenth Amendment which denied U.S. citizens the right to buy or drink alcoholic beverages. When he learned that the Government had hired fifteen hundred agents at $2,000 a year to enforce the law, he gave a snort of disgust. Big John knew from owning a restaurant that people liked to drink. He realized that soon the country would be wide open for rum-running.

Big John's empire, based on saloons and brothels, had grown soft with prosperity. To tighten it, he had sent to New York for Johnny Torrio, a coldly vicious killer whose boyhood chum had been Gyp the Blood of the Rosenthal killing. Torrio also saw the huge possibilities in rumrunning, but with the increased responsibilities it would bring he needed the help of an organizing genius like himself who could also act as a bodyguard. He remembered a tough Brooklyn youth named Alphonse "Scarface Al" Capone. Al turned out even better than Torrio hoped. As a soldier in the AEF he had fought at Belleau Wood and other battles. In them, he learned the efficacy of the machine gun.

Big John Colosimo's murder was never solved, thus establishing a pattern for most of Chicago's subsequent gangland murders. Perhaps his old friends had done away with him out of resentment over the importation of the grim talent from New York. Perhaps the New York talent did it—restive at his somewhat archaic methods in a totally new world. In any case, Johnny Torrio and Al Capone stood forth as masters of the lucrative mob territory known as the South Side.

In charge of the North Side was Dion O'Banion, onetime altar boy matured into safeblower and killer-for-hire. He was also a good husband and a devoted son. O'Banion had established gang headquarters over a florist shop which he bought as an investment. To the horror of his men, he became fascinated by the shop. The awesome gang leader, snipping flowers with zeal, slowly lost interest in the North Side booze business. In 1924, he had become so indifferent that he sold a large brewery to Torrio and Capone. Ten days later it was raided, costing the South Siders the full investment. Next, O'Banion's flower shop got an order for a large wreath. The boss himself worked on this special job, finishing just as three men walked in to claim it. They were quick-moving types, with dark, tight overcoats and snap-brim hats. One grabbed O'Banion by the hand, shook it warmly—and held on. The others pumped lead into Dion O'Banion.

O'Banion's funeral served notice on Chicago that gangland had taken over. It was glorious, with twenty-four cars of flowers and twenty thousand mourners. Some of the wreaths cost $5,000. Hymie Weiss, who inherited the North Side territory, was black with fury, vowing vengeance on Torrio and Capone. Torrio knew it and stayed home. Sixteen days after O'Banion's death, Torrio and his wife ventured to leave their apartment house by a back door. A big car roared by, with sawed-off shotguns firing garlic-tipped slugs. Three of these poison bullets hit Torrio. In the hospital he decided that the time had come

to serve a one-year jail sentence long hanging over his head. Johnny Torrio had never been called a coward, but he had what a reporter called "a blue-ribbon fright." From jail, a year later, he rushed to safety in his native Italy.

So Scarface Al Capone, still in his twenties, fearless in crisis but petulant in private life, was King of the South Side. Soon he was the most powerful man in Chicago, for where Torrio had been content to organize, Capone cleverly set out to merge underworld and politics. He took in $100,000,000 a year from his illegal liquor op-

The ruthless Johnny Torrio had imported Capone from Brooklyn as bodyguard. First they ran Chicago's South Side.

erations and paid out $30,000,000 in bribes and payoffs which reached from precinct level, to City Hall, to the State House. Capone took over the entire town of Cicero, Ill., opening it wide to gambling and vice. He operated his bootlegging empire from a fifty-room, two-floor headquarters in a midtown Chicago hotel. The setup included a gym for his bodyguards to keep in trim.

Pudgy Al sported a $50,000 diamond in his stickpin and drove around town in a $20,000 armor-plated limousine. His men rubbed out Hymie Weiss on a busy street. This elevated George "Bugs" Moran to the eminence of North Side leader. Moran was one of the gunmen who had shot Torrio and been so identified. But in

Dion O'Banion, (ABOVE) with his bride, bought a flower shop as a front for North Side bootlegging activities. Fascinated by the shop, he let rum-running lapse. Gunned down by Torrio hoods, his huge funeral (LOWER RIGHT) served notice on Chicago that gangland was king. His successor was Hymie Weiss (ABOVE RIGHT), who shot Torrio with garlic-tipped bullets.

Chicago's quaint way, he had never been arrested or tried. So, in 1926, he and Al Capone were the undisputed gang leaders of Chicago. . . .

Strange to relate, New York's gang lords never had the *elan* of Chicago's. Jack "Legs" Diamond, Owney Madden, Larry Fay, Big Frenchy De Mange, Waxey Gordon, Dutch Schultz—they all raked in millions in dollars and won fame in headlines. Yet they always seemed small about it. They backed nightclubs and during two cele-brated shoot-outs demolished the Club Abbey and the Hotsy Totsy Club. But they never rubbed out rivals in the heart of town, took over mid-town hotels, or entire suburbs like Cicero. Chi-cago gun toters made a hard try at looking flashy and dapper, but in New York Dutch Schultz grumbled, "Silk shirts! A guy's a sucker to spend fifteen or twenty bucks on a silk shirt. Hell, I can buy a good shirt for two bucks."

There, perhaps, lay the difference.

New York lagged behind Chicago in organized lawlessness, but what-ever the locale gangland killings were alike. (BELOW), *New York's Dutch Schultz filled with lead in the traditional manner.*

161

Escorted into jail by a matron, Ruth Snyder (LEFT) had gotten as far from suburbia as a housewife could. Judd Gray (ABOVE), her accomplice and lover, smoked nervously while being booked in the murder of Mr. Snyder.

1927

47. "MOMSIE, MOMSIE, FOR GOD'S SAKE, HELP!"

The Snyder-Gray murder—a writer said—was a cheap crime involving cheap people. Many consider it a nadir-point in American culture and taste. Yet citizens of the thrill-hungry Twenties devoured every sordid detail, and elevated Ruth Snyder and Judd Gray to heights of notoriety.

It all began in 1925 when Ruth Brown Snyder, a discontented Queens Village, L.I., housewife, met corset salesman Henry Judd Gray at lunch in New York. Ruth, thirty-two, was a tall, blonde Nordic type, whose granite good looks indicated latent power. Judd Gray, thirty-four, was short and unprepossessing, his cleft chin and heavy horn-rim glasses giving him the look of a startled rabbit. Yet on first meeting a vast sexual attraction flared between the dissimilar pair. Mrs.

The Snyder home in Queens Village, L.I., hardly looked like the den of what tabloids called the Tiger Woman.

Snyder's husband was art editor of the magazine *Motor Boating* and the couple had a nine-year-old daughter, Lorraine. Ruth and Judd met whenever possible and often Lorraine dangled feet in a hotel lobby while the amorous pair romanced upstairs. Sometimes Judd went to Queens Village in the daytime. There the two used Lorraine's bed.

Slowly Ruth Snyder changed from a sex-obsessed woman to a female with plans. Bored with a loveless marriage, she began to see salvation ahead. She told Judd that her husband mistreated her and must be killed. He objected, but she persisted. The two used baby talk in which she was "Momsie" or "Momie," while he was "Bud" or "Lover Boy." Judd Gray took to drink, becoming so inured to Prohibition rotgut that he could down nearly a pint at a swallow.

"Momsie" begged, cajoled, argued, threatened. Still "Lover Boy" refused. "Do you realize what it would mean in the eyes of God," he asked naively. But when she tried to poison Albert Snyder, Gray gave in. He promised to enter her Queens Village house by the back door on the night of Saturday, March 19, 1927, when the Snyders, including Lorraine, would be at a late party. Judd promised to hide in a spare room, where Ruth had put a sashweight, rubber gloves, chloroform and other utensils of murder.

On the morning of the 19th, Gray was in Syracuse on a corset-selling trip. He took the train to New York and traveled the fifteen miles to Queens Village in a bus. He walked around for an hour, stopping under street lights to take copious swigs from a flask of Prohibition hooch. It was as if he wished to be seen and perhaps arrested for breaching the law of the land. Nobody noticed him and at last he entered the house and went upstairs, to crouch in the dark room taking more swigs of hooch. The family returned at 2 A.M. and Ruth opened the door a crack. "Are you there, Bud, dear?" she whispered.

Shortly she was back, dressed in a slip, and the two kissed and clung together for an hour. Then Gray took up the five-pound sashweight from under a pillow. Ruth picked up the other objects and led the way to the master bedroom where Albert Snyder slept with bedclothes over his head. The two stood on opposite sides of the bed as Gray raised the sashweight to bring it down clumsily on the sleeping figure. Gray was no muscleman—the blow hurt rather than stunned. Albert Snyder roared up, trying to seize his sudden attacker. "Momsie, Momsie, for God's sake, help!" Judd cried. Mrs. Snyder angrily reached across the bed, grabbed the sashweight, and brought it down on her husband's head.

The Snyder-Gray killing was not only sordid, but inept. Damon Runyon called it the Dumbbell Murder—"because it was so dumb." After murdering Snyder, the two went downstairs for a chat and drinks. Then they mussed up the house to indicate robbery. After this, Judd loosely bound Ruth's hands and left. She called police, greeting them with histrionics borrowed from Theda Bara, Nita Naldi, and other screen vamps. Police suspected her from the first. On slight pressure she confessed, blaming Judd. By this time

A few hours before the murder, Judd Gray sent birthday greetings to Momsie. On envelope is his handwriting which he disguised in all notes sent to Ruth.

164

the corset salesman was back in Syracuse. When detectives arrived he denied leaving the hotel on the murder night, but in the wastebasket lay his railroad ticket stub.

The trial of the pair in Long Island City became another gaudy circus, with ace reporters, sob sisters, feature writers, photographers, milling crowds, and the Western Union switchboard from the Hall-Mills trial. Though the crime had been blunt as the murder weapon, the trial could have been written by a dramatist: Blonde Mrs. Snyder, dressed in black, kept twisting her pearls until drops of blood appeared; Gray, meek and broken, came to amazing life on the witness stand to paint a devastating picture of a man trapped by a scheming woman; at one point in his testimony, Ruth let out an unearthly shriek; as a witness she was at first haughty, but left the stand confused and sobbing; the lawyers squabbled so much that there seemed to be three trials going on. Evidence against the pair was overwhelming. Nonetheless, Ruth and Judd were stunned at the verdict of guilty.

This was May 9, 1927. Eleven days later Charles A. Lindbergh, the Lone Eagle, flew the Atlantic. It was the end of an era. A nation that had been wallowing in the gutter with Ruth and Judd lifted eyes upward to purge itself in wild worship of Lucky Lindy. Attention briefly swung back to the murderous pair on the night of January 12, 1928, when Ruth and Judd were electrocuted in Sing Sing. Then they were forgotten.

A Daily News *photographer, a tiny camera strapped to his ankle, snapped this photo of Ruth Snyder in the electric chair as the death-current surged, recording the gruesome penalty.*

165

Dear Daddy and Mother:

*I wish I could come home.
I think I'll die if I have to
be like this much longer.
Wont someone tell me why
all this had to happen to me.
Daddy please do what the
man tells your or he'll kill
me if youdon't.*

*Your loving daughter
Marion Parker.*

*P.S. Please Daddy.
I want to come home tonight*

With the kidnaper standing over her, 12-year-old Marian Parker wrote this note to her parents. The case horrified the nation, began the biggest manhunt in West Coast history.

1927

48. MURDER FOR A HIGHER EDUCATION

Edward Hickman was a short, curly-haired Los Angeles youth. Twenty years old in 1927, he seemed to derive his ideas of living from the Leopold-Loeb case.

The young man needed $1,500 for college tuition—or thought he did. For several days in early December, 1927, he toured expensive neighborhoods until he spotted a residence that particularly impressed him. He learned that its owner was Perry Parker, prospering businessman and adoring father of Marjorie and Marian, 12-year-old twins. Hickman decided that Parker would gladly pay $1,500 to get his daughters back. The only hitch was the difficulty of kidnaping twins.

Fate played into his hands as Marjorie got sick and stayed home from school one afternoon. Hickman drove up to the junior high-school playground and called to Marian, "There's trouble at home—your father sent me to get you." In those days little girls were seldom warned to distrust curly-haired strangers. Marian got into the car beside him. She was a bright-looking child with a sunny disposition, but to Hickman this counted for nothing. He dictated a note which a terrified girl wrote to her father, then cold-

Little Marian was selected because her father so obviously adored her and her twin sister. Kidnaper reasoned such a man would unhesitatingly pay ransom.

bloodedly strangled her and sliced off her legs with a pocket knife. A doctor later stated that the unlucky child had died of sheer fright.

Like Chicago's Thrill Killers, Hickman considered himself an outstanding intellect. He bombarded Perry Parker with egotistical ransom notes signed The Fox or Fate, each decorated at the top with the word DEATH in fancy, printed letters. The notes told Parker his daughter would be returned on payment of $1,500.

At first Parker worked with police. Then he decided to act on his own. Over the telephone a meeting in a wooded development was arranged. Parker drove up beside Hickman's parked car. "Is my daughter alive?" he called. The Fox lifted up Marian's body, wrapped in a blanket, the face visible. Marian appeared asleep or drugged. "Give me the money and I'll leave her down the road a way," he instructed. Parker tossed the

With Marian dead, the kidnaper wrote his own notes, heading them DEATH and signing them FATE. "Fox is my name," this begins, "Very sly you know."

167

ΔΕΑΤΗ

P.M.Parker:
Use good judgment. You are the loser. Do This. Secure 75 - $20 gold certificates - U.S. Currency - 1500 dollars - at once. KEEP THEM ON YOUR PERSON. GO ABOUT YOUR DAILY BUSINESS AS USUAL. LEAVE OUT POLICE AND DETECTIVES. MAKE NO PUBLIC NOTICE. KEEP THIS AFFAIR PRIVATE. MAKE NO SEARCH.
fullfilling these terms with the transfer of the currency will secure the return of the girl.
FAILURE TO COMPLY WITH THESE REQUESTS MEANS - NO ONE WILL EVER SEE THE GIRL AGAIN. except the angels in heaven.
The affair must end one way or the other within 3 days. 72 HRS.
YOU WILL RECEIVE FURTHER NOTICE,
But the terms Remain the Same.

FATE

If YOU WANT AID AGAINST ME ASK GOD NOT MAN.

United Press International Photo

Perry Parker received daily notes from FATE. *"Leave out police and detectives," this warns.*

money in the murderer's car. Hickman drove ahead a block, then stopped to place Marian's wrapped body on the ground. The father rushed to the child, opened the blanket—and never was able to describe in his own words what he saw.

California reeled in horror as the search for Hickman fanned up and down the West Coast. On December 23rd, he was captured in Seattle and as his train proceeded southward public shock seemed to recede. Crowds gathered at every stop, while in Los Angeles thousands lined the route from train to jail. But these were not vengeful crowds. Rather they were curious folk out for the sight of a murderer. Evincing neither anger nor hostility, they showed only a passive, gloating curiosity. Could it be, moralists wondered, that the lurid headline-crimes of the Roaring Twenties had left a public drained of emotion, completely jaded. . . .

While crowds strained to glimpse him, Edward Hickman acted out a pattern of the criminal psychopath which in time became more familiar as knowledge of psychiatry grew. On the train from Seattle he tried twice to kill himself. In jail, he bragged of other murders. He first claimed an accomplice in Marian's murder, then suddenly admitted doing it alone.

This was the Tabloid Age in Los Angeles as well as New York, and photographers had easy access to the jail. Hickman preened before them, expressing a preference for the pictures of his head and shoulders which hid his short stature. To the sob sisters who accompanied the photographers he poured out the story of a misspent life and eagerly agreed with the suggestion that too many movies had caused his downfall.

Left alone he was prey to fits of despair and self-hate. He confided in a fellow prisoner that his only hope lay in feigning insanity. Then he described exactly how he planned to do this. The prosecution put the other prisoner on the stand and Hickman was finished—if he ever had a chance. Found guilty of murder on February 4, 1928, he was hanged at San Quentin.

FATE *turned out to be Edward Hickman, age 20, who kidnaped Marian to get money for college—or so he said.*

United Press International Photo

168

49. THE END OF MR. BIG

Gambler Arnold Roth-stein was the autocrat of the underworld, which called him Mr. Big.

Broadway gave many names to master-gambler Arnold Rothstein. He was Mr. Big, Mr. A, The Brain, The Man Uptown, The Man to See, and The Big Bankroll. Most intimate was A.R. Yet none of them did justice to a figure who could have stepped from the pages of a superior crime novel.

Broadway's Mr. Big was the son of a man so respected in New York's Jewish community that he was called Rothstein the Just. Arnold never thought of following in his father's footsteps.

From the moment the boy learned about dice, cards, and betting, he was a gambler. He had a mind like an adding machine, nerves of tempered steel, and a heart of ice. So equipped, he rapidly made his way in Manhattan. At twenty he was a part owner of a plush gambling house, remaining there until his partner discovered Arnold cheating him. In 1912, he was a friend of the murdered Herman Rosenthal. In 1920, he attained national fame for allegedly fixing the World Series the previous fall. In 1922, he calmly sacrificed his friend Nicky Arnstein (see page 131) to the law. He bet heavily on top sporting events and usually tried to bribe a participant. "A.R. has a fix in," became a familiar whisper around town. But his supreme moment came with Prohibition. When New York's bootleggers began to shoot it out in the Chicago manner, A.R. stepped in and persuaded the boys to carve the big city into

computerlike mind. Back at 49th, he went into Lindy's, his nighttime headquarters. First he phoned the bets he had taken to a bookkeeper in his office on 57th Street. Then he sat down, ordered black coffee, and took more bets.

A.R. always carried at least $200,000 in crisp thousand-dollar bills, and would lend to anyone. In that lay the secret of his political power. Judges, lawyers, politicians, gangsters, stage stars rushed to him in moments of financial stress. But the day the money was due Rothstein expected it back. For years the psychotic killer Jack "Legs" Diamond stood at A.R.'s elbow to make sure the money was returned, together with sizable interest or some political favor.

All this made Mr. Big wealthy, with two limousines, a Fifth Avenue home, and valuable real estate holdings. His only love was gambling, though he had an attractive wife and a series of glittering show-girl mistresses. He wore $45-a-pair shoes—those Broadway strolls were hard on the arches!—and $250 suits. He truly looked the part of master-gambler. At forty-six, he was

The room from which the trail of blood led was on the third floor of the Park Central Hotel, Seventh Avenue and 55th Street.

The dying Rothstein was found in the service entrance of the hotel, clutching his fatal wound.

lucrative areas of influence. For this he exacted huge reward.

Rothstein would bet on anything. Each night his chauffeur let him off at Broadway and 49th Street. From there, he strolled down to 42nd Street and back. Every few feet he stopped to accept bets, setting the odds instantly with his

soft-spoken, grammatically acceptable, and trim. A strong jaw aided his reputation for ruthlessness and milk-white skin increased his sleekness. He had few friends, but that was the way A.R. wanted it.

Suddenly, in 1928, the tensions of a gambler's life caught up with him. His main confidants were

170

Lindy waiters and to them he complained that his mind was growing fuzzy, making it hard to figure odds. In the pre-dawn card games he dearly loved Rothstein's hands shook and his bets were uncertain. A doctor might have ordered a rest, but The Man to See was a colossal egotist. Doctors—who needed 'em?

His whole judgment seemed to be affected. Why else, then, would he stay in the big poker game that ran from September 8 to September 10, 1928. . . .

A.R. had begun playing with a group assembled by his friend George "Hump" McManus.

George "Hump" McManus, genial gambler, longtime Rothstein pal and occupant of the hotel room, was arrested for the murder. But the case was so weak that the judge tossed it out.

"Nigger Nate" Raymond, West Coast gambler, had cleaned out Rothstein's purse at poker.

Most of the other players were familiar, but two young strangers from the West—"Titanic" Thompson and "Nigger Nate" Raymond—were also dealt in. A.R. first became irritated when these two outlanders failed to recognize his importance. He played like a fumbling amateur and, as annoyance mounted, accused the Westerners of cheating. At the same time, he tried to be the Big Bankroll, raising stakes from hundreds into thousands. After two days and nights, the weary players began falling out, leaving only Rothstein and Nigger Nate, a man Mr. Big now hated. Rothstein, the loser, made a final challenge of $50,000 bet on a single high-card draw. Nigger Nate agreed—and won. Face livid, A.R. leaped to his feet. In all, he had lost $320,000 to the group. "I'll pay off in a day or two," he snarled.

171

A cab driver found the gun that killed Rothstein across the street from the hotel. Smashed, it was tossed from an upper story. The photo at right poses questions that nagged the police.

"I don't carry that sort of dough under my fingernails." But, of course, he did.

Twenty-four hours later he was back at his Lindy table. The big game had been crooked, he informed the waiters. He'd never settle. The Main Stem reeled—the great A.R. welshing on a bet!

Over following weeks word came from various sources that payment would be appreciated. "I won't pay a cent," he snapped. "The game was rigged." On the night of November 4th—it was the eve of the Hoover-Smith election and A.R. had bet a packet on Hoover—he appeared at Lindy's. He sat sipping coffee and taking bets until summoned to the telephone. "I'm going up to the Park Central to see Hump McManus," he said after taking the call.

Half an hour later the great Arnold Rothstein stood in the service entrance of the Park Central Hotel, clutching his mid-section. Blood from a bullet wound oozed through his fingers. It had left a trickling red trail down the service stairs from Room 349, occupied by George McManus. Rothstein told the service elevator operator to get him a cab, but the man got an ambulance instead. At Polyclinic Hospital detectives urged Rothstein to name his killer. He raised a finger cryptically to his lips and died.

Everyone but George McManus had an alibi for the murder night. Nigger Nate Raymond had the best—he was in bed with a lush young bride. In time, McManus was placed on trial but evidence against him proved so flimsy that the judge dismissed the charge.

Rothstein's murderer was never named, but Broadway wise guys still say they know who killed Mr. Big.

172

United Press International Photo

This innocent facade concealed the headquarters of the George "Bugs" Moran gang, enemies of Al Capone. The St. Valentine's Day Massacre, gangland's worst killing, took place inside.

50. THE ST. VALENTINE'S DAY MASSACRE

At ten-thirty on the morning of February 14, 1929—St. Valentine's Day—a big black Cadillac touring car drew up before the S.M.C. Cartage Company, at 2122 North Clark Street, in Chicago. The car had an official, police-special look, with an alarm bell on the running board and gun rack in the rear. The impression of officialdom was increased as two men in what appeared to be police uniforms alighted. They were followed by two others in plain clothes who might be detectives.

The S.M.C. Cartage Company lay just a mile from Chicago's City Hall. Yet those in the neighborhood who saw the official-looking car carefully tried not to notice it. This was the heart of Chicago's North Side, bailiwick of George "Bugs" Moran, who had inherited the O'Banion-Weiss mantle as arch foe of Scarface Al Capone. Nothing ever happened in front of S.M.C. Cartage, but much went on in the rear. Heavy trucks moved in and out late at night, and gossip said they unloaded liquor which had just been hijacked. More, a lot of the liquor was hi-jacked from Al Capone. One of the men often seen around the premises at 2122 Clark Street was Bugs Moran himself. He was reputed to feel that Capone was slipping. Now, perhaps, he could muscle into the lucrative South Side.

So the neighbors did not crowd around to watch as the law entered S.M.C. But they listened. Shortly a series of metallic *ra-ta-tats* were heard, followed by two heavy detonations. Almost immediately the two cops reappeared holding guns on two men whose hands were held high—later it was decided that these were the same two who had resembled detectives going in. The four got in the big car and drove away. Only then did one neighbor summon nerve to peer inside. He came out whitefaced. "The place is full of dead men," he reported.

173

Quizzical Bugs Moran (LEFT) decided that Capone was slipping, began hijacking his booze deliveries. His seven top aides (ABOVE) were waiting for Moran on St. Valentine's morning when they became the victims of the mass slaying.

What the man had seen was the terrible St. Valentine's Day massacre which brought Chicago's years of gang war to a horrendous climax. "The most horrifying crime in the history of Prohibition," author Edward Dean Sullivan calls it. Inside the drab building, seven members of the Moran gang had been awaiting the arrival of their boss. Moran was late. One gang member bore a resemblance to Moran and paid his leader the tribute of dressing like him. This man had just entered, and apparently the killers mistook him for Moran.

When the phony cops got inside, they whipped open their coats to produce two machine guns and two sawed-off shotguns. The seven Moran gangsters were directed to stand with faces to the brick wall, hands upstretched. In this position they were mowed down by machine-gun fire which moved undeviatingly back and forth between ears and thigh. The two final detonations came from a shotgun used for good measure on two victims. When at last real police arrived one gangster was still alive, though his body held fourteen slugs. "Who did it?" a police sergeant demanded. "It's getting darker, Sarge, so long," he whispered, and rolled over dead.

At the exact instant of the seven-man slaughter, Al Capone was in Miami closeted with the local D.A. The gang lord had been spending much time in Florida lately, living in luxury in rented mansions and finding the climate to his liking. Nonetheless, he was immediately suspected of ordering the St. Valentine's Day killings. Bugs Moran, for once on the side of virtue, summed up when he said, "Only the Capone gang kills that way."

No arrest was ever made for the St. Valentine's murders, although police came to believe that two of the killers were John Scalise and Albert Anselmi, Capone lieutenants. Before any evidence could be collected these two were also dead. If Scalise and Anselmi had done the job, they bungled badly. First, they failed to kill Moran. Second, they committed a crime which aroused widespread public indignation. Al Capone now made a quick return to Chicago. The story is that he pretended to ignore the bungling. He congratulated the two gunmen and threw a party in their honor. At it, he got the two men knee-walking drunk, then personally beat them to death with a baseball bat.

If he did this the lionlike Al Capone was short-lived. Like Johnny Torrio before him, Capone began to suffer from a blue-ribbon fright. Back in Miami he talked of the wastefulness of gang killings. Using his immense power he convened

174

a summit meeting of Chicago crime-lords in Atlantic City. One who attended, with bodyguard,
was Bugs Moran. Results of this choice gathering
were not comforting to Al and—once more like
Torrio—he decided that jail was the safest place
for him to pass the next year. He went to Philadelphia, where he and bodyguard "Big" Cline
dawdled conspicuously around town until arrested for carrying concealed weapons. In jail,
Al philosophized, "It's a tough life I lead. I

*"Only the Capone gang kills this way," mut-
tered Moran on seeing the corpses. He himself
was alive only because he was late.*

haven't had any peace of mind for years. Every
minute I am in danger of death."

Scarface Al may have thought a prison sentence might take the heat off him. It didn't. In
Chicago, a group of prominent citizens banded
together as the Secret Six determined to put him
behind bars. As Chicagoans, the Six knew better

175

than to expect help on City or State level. They called on the Federal Government to trap Capone on tax evasion. Scarface Al—who reputedly kept a personal $30,000,000 from his annual $100,000,000 take—had never filed a return or paid a cent of tax. He kept no records, piously calling himself an honest businessman. To prove its case the Government had to tie Capone concretely to his bootleg millions. In 1932, he was brought to trial, convicted, and sentenced to eleven years in prison. But already Al Capone was under another terrible sentence. Among his enterprises was a flock of lush bawdy houses. Al had behaved brutishly to some of the girls, one of whom achieved a subtle revenge. She infected Al Capone with syphilis. Not until it was too late to cure did the greatest of gang lords learn this. He served his prison sentence, part of it on Alcatraz, then went back to Miami. He died in 1947, aged 48, doddering and dimwitted from paresis.

When the police suspected John Scalise and Albert Anselmi (ABOVE) of masterminding the massacre, the two Capone lieutenants mysteriously died. Capone, possibly their murderer, escaped federal conviction until 1932 by only allowing his surface affairs, such as fishing off Florida, to show.

BIBLIOGRAPHY

Boswell, Charles and Thompson, Lewis, *The Girl in Lover's Lane*. Greenwich, Conn., Gold Medal Books, 1952

Busch, Francis X., *Enemies of the State*. Indianapolis and New York, The Bobbs Merrill Company, 1954

———— *Prisoners at the Bar*. Indianapolis and New York, The Bobbs Merrill Company, 1952

Carr, William H. A., *Hollywood Tragedy*. New York, Lancer Books, 1962

Collins, Frederick L., *Glamorous Sinners*. New York, Ray Long and Richard R. Smith, 1932

Collins, Ted (ed.), *New York Murders*. New York, Duell, Sloan & Pearce, 1944

Cook, Fred J., *Sacco-Vanzetti: The Missing Fingerprints*. (*Nation*, December 22, 1962, pp 442–51)

De la Torre, Lillian, *The Truth about Belle Gunness*. New York, Gold Medal Books, 1955

Donovan, Robert J., *The Assassins*. New York, Harper & Brothers, 1952

Franz, Eleanor W., *The Tragedy of the North Woods*. (*New York Folklore Quarterly*, Summer 1948, pp 85–97)

Harlow, Alvin F., *Murders Not Quite Solved*. New York, Julian Messner, Inc., 1938

House, Brant, *Crimes That Shocked America*. New York, Ace Books, 1961

Hynd, Alan, *Con Man*. New York, Paperback Library, 1961

Guild, Leo, *The Fatty Arbuckle Case*. New York, Paperback Library, 1962

Katcher, Leo, *The Big Bankroll*. New York, Harper & Brothers, 1958

Klein, Alexander (ed.), *Double Dealers*. Philadelphia and New York, J. B. Lippincott & Company, 1958

Jackson, Joseph Henry (ed.), *The Portable Murder Book*. New York, The Viking Press, 1945

———— *San Francisco Murders*. New York, Duell, Sloan & Pearce, 1947

Langford, Gerald, *The Murder of Stanford White*. Indianapolis and New York, The Bobbs Merrill Company, 1962

Levy, Newman, *The Nan Patterson Case*. New York, Simon & Schuster, 1959

Lord, Walter, *The Good Years*. New York, Harper & Brothers, 1960

McDade, Thomas, *Annals of Murder*, a Bibliography. Norman, University of Oklahoma Press, 1961

Madison, Charles A., *Critics and Crusaders*. New York, Henry Holt & Co., 1948

Morris, Joe Alex, *What A Year!* New York, Harper & Brothers, 1956

Musmanno, Michael A., *Was Sacco Guilty?* (*New Republic*, March 2, 1963, pp 25–30)

Pasley, Fred, *Al Capone*. New York, Ives Washburn, 1930

Pearson, Edmund L., *More Studies in Murder*. New York, Harrison Smith & Robert Haas, 1936

———— *Murder at Smutty Nose*. New York and Garden City, Doubleday, Page & Co., 1927

———— *Studies in Murder*. New York, Macmillan Company, 1926

Radin, Edward D., *Lizzie Borden, the Untold Story*. New York, Simon & Schuster, 1961

Root, Jonathan, *One Night in July*. New York, Coward McCann Inc., 1961

Runyon, Damon, *Trials and Other Tribulations*. Philadelphia and New York, J. B. Lippincott & Company, 1926

Sann, Paul, *The Lawless Decade*. New York, Crown Publishers Inc., 1957

Stern, Philip Van Doren, *The Man Who Killed Lincoln*. New York, Random House, 1935

Stone, Irving, *Clarence Darrow for the Defense*. New York, Doubleday & Co., 1941

Sullivan, Edward Dean, *Rattling the Cup on Chicago Crime*. New York, Vanguard Press, 1929

Swanberg, W. A., *Jim Fisk*. New York, Charles Scribner's Sons, 1959

Van Every, Edward, *Sins of America*. New York, Frederick A. Stokes, 1931

———— *Sins of New York*, New York, Frederick A. Stokes, 1930

Young, Art, *On My Way*. New York, Horace Liveright, 1928

*

Magazines and Newspapers: *American Mercury, Collier's, Detective World, True, Vanderbilt Law Review*, New Bedford (Mass.) *Standard Times*, New York *Daily News*, New York *World*

INDEX

Altgeld, John Peter, 34, 35
An American Tragedy, 80
Anarchists, 33–6, 121–4, 130
Anderson, George "Dutch," 155–7
Anselmi, Albert, 174
Arlington, Billy, 84
Arnold, Dorothy, 101–3
Arnstein, Nicky, 131–2
Arbuckle, Roscoe "Fatty," 133–5, 136
Becker, Police Lieut. Charles, 104–6
Benchley, Robert, 124
Bender family, 11–14
Bender, Miss Kate, 11–14
Berkman, Alexander, 35, 36
Billings, Warren, 116, 117
Blaine, James G., 25, 26
Booth, John Wilkes, 8–10
Borden, Andrew J., 40–1
Borden, Emma, 40, 41, 42
Borden, Lizzie, 39–42
Botkin, Cordelia, 55–6
Brentano's, 101
Brice, Fannie, 131, 132
Broun, Heywood, 124
Brown, Grace "Billy," 80–2
Burns Detective Agency, 96
Cafe Metropole, 106
Capone, Alphonse "Scarface Al," 158–61, 173–6
Carnegie, Andrew, 35, 68, 69, 70, 71
Cary, Detective Inspector, 127
Chadwick, Cassie, 68–71
Chamberlin, W. J., 35
Chapman, Gerald, 155–7
Colosimo, Big John, 158, 159
Coolidge, Governor Calvin, 119
Corbett, Boston, 10
Cornish, Harry, 60, 61, 62
Czolgosz, Leon, 65, 66
Darrow, Clarence, 34, 94–7, 153, 154
Daugherty, Harry, 147, 148, 149
de la Torre, Lillian, 41
Delmas, Delphin, 79
De Russey's Lane, 139, 140, 141
Diamond, Jack "Legs," 161, 171
Dos Passos, John, 124
Dreiser, Theodore, 80
Dreyfus, Mrs. Aurelia, 145, 146
Doheny, Edward L., 148, 150

Dunning, John Presley, 55, 56
Durrant, Theo, 47–50
Elwell, Joseph B., 125–7
Emanuel Baptist Church, 48, 49
Emerson, Ralph Waldo, 31
Fall, Albert B., 140–50
Fallon, Bill, 131, 132
Ferber, Edna, 84
Fisk, Jim, 15–18, 27
Florodora Sextette, 72
Ford brothers, 29, 30
Ford's Theater, 7, 9
Frank, Leo, 108–11
Frank Leslie's Weekly, 39
Franks, Bobby, 152, 153
Freud, Dr. Sigmund, 76, 136
Frick, Henry Clay, 35, 36
Garden City Cathedral, 22, 24
Garfield, President James, 25–8
Gaynor, Mayor William, 98
Gibson, Mrs. Jane "Pig Woman," 141, 142, 143
Gillette, Chester, 80–2
Gilligan Edmund, 129
Goldsborough, Fitzhugh Coyle, 99
Gould, Jay, 16
Grand Hotel, 57, 58
Gray, Judd, 163–5
Griscom, George Jr., 102, 103
Guerin, Webster, 85
Guimares, Alberto, 145, 156
Guiteau, Charles, 25–8
Guldensuppe, Willie, 51–3
Gunness, Belle, 86–90
Gyp the Blood, 105, 106, 159
Hall, Rev. Edward Wheeler, 139–43
Hall, Mrs. Frances Stevens, 139–43
Harding, President Warren, 147, 148, 149
Harper's Weekly, 35, 36
Havernack, Frank, 156
Haymarket Bombing, 33–5
Hays, Will H., 138
Helgelien, Asle, 88, 90
Herold, David, 9, 10
Hickman, Edward, 166–9
Holmes, Harry Howard, 43–6
Homestead Strike, 35, 36
Howells, William Dean, 34
James, Frank, 29–32

James, Jesse, 29–32
Jerome, William Travers, 79
Kendrick, Baynard, 59
Kennedy, Dr. Samuel, 57, 58, 59
Kidnapping, 19–21, 166–68
King, Dot, 144–6
Knickerbocker Athletic Club, 60, 61
Kraus, Viola, 126
Lamont, Blanche, 48, 49, 50
Lamphere, Ray, 86, 88, 89, 90
Leishman, John, 35
Leopold, Nathan, 151–4
Lewishohn, Mr. & Mrs. Walter, 126
Lincoln, President Abraham, 7–10, 25
Lindbergh, Charles A., 165
Lindy's, 170, 171
Lingg, Louis, 34, 35
Loeb, Richard, 151–4
Loeber, Charles, 156, 157
Longfellow, Henry Wadsworth, 4, 31
Los Angeles *Times,* 95
Lowell, A. Lawrence, 124
McDonald, Dora Feldman, 83–5
McDonald, Michael Cassius, 83–5
McKinley, President William, 63–5
McLean, Edward B., 150
McManus, George "Hump," 171, 172
McMasters, William, 120
McNamara brothers, 95, 96, 97
Madison Square Garden, 77, 78
Mansfield, Josie, 16–18
Massachusetts Medical College, 3
Mendham, Maurice B., 57
Millington, Frank C., 37–8
Millington, Mary Avery, 37–8
Mills, Mrs. Eleanor, 139–43
Minter, Mary Miles, 137
Mitchell, J. Kearsley, 145, 146
Molineux, Roland, 60–2
Mooney, Tom, 115–17
Moore, Governor A. Harry, 143
Moran, George "Bugs," 159, 173, 174
Morelli Gang, 124
Morgan, J. P. & Co., 129, 130
Mudd, Dr. Samuel, 9
Murder Castle, 44, 45, 46
Mussolini, Benito, 120
Nack, Mrs. Augusta, 51–3
Nesbit, Evelyn, 77, 79
New York *Journal,* 51, 53
New York *Mirror,* 142, 143
New York *World,* 51, 55, 59
Normand, Mabel, 137, 138
O'Banion, Dion, 159, 160
Otis, Harrison Gray, 94
Pan-American Exposition, 63
Park Central Hotel, 172
Parker, Dorothy, 124
Parker, Marian, 167–9
Patterson, Nan, 72–5
Parkman, Dr. George, 3–6
Payne, Philip, 142

Pearson, Edmund Lester, 42
Phagan, Mary, 108–11
Phillips, David Graham, 99–100
Pinkerton Detectives, 29, 35
Pitzel, Ben, 46
Police Gazette, 31, 47, 49
Ponzi, Charles, 118–20
Radin, Edward, 42
Rappe, Virginia, 134, 135
Raymond, "Nigger Nate," 171, 172
Reynolds, Dolly, 57–9
Rogers, Earl, 97
Roosevelt, President Theodore, 66, 77
Rose, "Billiard Ball Jack," 105, 106
Rosenthal, Herman "Beansie," 105, 106
Ross, Charley, 19–21
Rothstein, Arnold, 132, 169–72
Runyon, Damon, 164
Sacco, Nicola, 121–4
Scalise, John, 174
Schultz, Dutch, 161
Shean, Walter, 157
Sherman, Lowell, 134
Show Boat, 84
Sibley, Frank J., 124
Simpson, Alexander, 143
Sinclair, Harry B., 148, 150
Sing Sing Death House, 62
Snead, Ocey, 91–3
Synder, Ruth, 162–5
Soule College, 92, 93
Spies, August, 34, 35
Steffens, Lincoln, 97
Stevens, Willie, 140, 141, 142, 143
Stewart, A. T., 22–4
Stewart, Police Chief Michael, 122, 123
Stokes, Ned, 16–18
Sullivan, Bridget, 41, 42
Taylor, William Desmond, 136–8
Teapot Dome, 147–50
Thaw, Harry K., 76–9
Thayer, Judge Webster, 124
Thorn, Martin, 52, 53
Torrio, Johnny, 158, 159, 174
Trude, Asa, 85
Tweed, Boss, 16
Vanzetti, Bartolomeo, 121–4
Waldo, Rhonelander, 104
Walker, Mayor James J., 117
Wall Street Explosion, 128–30
Walling, Police Chief, 20, 23
Wardlaw, Virginia, 92, 93
Webster, Dr. John W., 3–6
Weil, Joseph "Yellow Kid," 113–14
Weiss, Hymie, 159, 160
Westervelt, William, 20, 21, 23
White, Stanford, 76–9
Whitman, Charles S., 105, 106, 107
Williams, Minnie, 49, 50
Yerkes, Charles T., 84
Young, Caesar, 74–5
Ziegfeld's Midnight Frolic, 126